Guide to Electronic Resource Management

Guide to Electronic Resource Management

Sheri V. T. Ross and Sarah W. Sutton

LIBRARIES
UNLIMITED™

An Imprint of ABC-CLIO, LLC

Santa Barbara, California • Denver, Colorado

Library of Congress Cataloging-in-Publication Data

Names: Ross, Sheri V. T., author. | Sutton, Sarah W., author.
Title: Guide to electronic resource management / Sheri V. T. Ross and
    Sarah W. Sutton.
Description: Santa Barbara, CA : Libraries Unlimited, [2016] |
    Includes bibliographical references and index.
Identifiers: LCCN 2015037581 | ISBN 9781440839580 (paperback) |
    ISBN 9781440839597 (ebook)
Subjects: LCSH: Libraries—Special collections—Electronic information
    resources. | Electronic information resources—Management. | BISAC:
    LANGUAGE ARTS & DISCIPLINES / Library & Information Science /
    Cataloging & Classification. | LANGUAGE ARTS & DISCIPLINES /
    Library & Information Science / General.
Classification: LCC Z692.C65 G85 2016 | DDC 025.1—dc23
LC record available at http://lccn.loc.gov/2015037581

ISBN: 978-1-4408-3958-0
EISBN: 978-1-4408-3959-7

20 19 18 17 16   1 2 3 4 5

This book is also available on the World Wide Web as an eBook.
Visit www.abc-clio.com for details.

Libraries Unlimited
An Imprint of ABC-CLIO, LLC

ABC-CLIO, LLC
130 Cremona Drive, P.O. Box 1911
Santa Barbara, California 93116-1911

This book is printed on acid-free paper ∞

Manufactured in the United States of America

Contents

7 MANAGING ACCESS AND DISCOVERY 93

8 ASSESSING ELECTRONIC RESOURCES 105

9 PRESERVING ELECTRONIC RESOURCES 119

Preface

This textbook developed as a result of need, as many do. Both of us teach electronic resources management in master's level library science programs and struggled to find an up-to-date text. Part of the challenge, of course, is rapid change, which is one of the hallmarks of work with electronic resources in libraries and other information agencies. With that challenge in mind, we have created our own textbook, a distillation of what we strive to teach our students in order to prepare them for work with electronic resources in libraries.

In addition to the clear advantages and disadvantages the electronic resources present for libraries and their customers, there are several aspects of work with electronic resources that are simply different from the work required for their physical counterparts. Most of these differences stem from the increased complexity of both the resources themselves and the work required in order to acquire, organize, provide access to, maintain, troubleshoot, and preserve them. These activities are the focus of this textbook.

Chapters 2 and 3 set up the stage for and describe the context in which librarians manage electronic resources. In Chapter 2, we will address the notion of content, including the environments in which electronic content is produced, content providers, and the economics of digital content. In Chapter 3, we address standards, recommended practices and professional guidelines, and their impact on the management of electronic resources in libraries. In Chapters 4 through 8, we dig into the processes and procedures involved in the day-to-day management of electronic resources: acquisitions (Chapter 4), licenses and contracts (Chapter 5), providing access through authentication (Chapter 6), providing access through linking and discovery (Chapter 7), and assessing and evaluating electronic resources (Chapter 8). Chapter 9 describes the challenges for preserving electronic content, and Chapter 10 provides an overview of the process of scholarly communication as it influences the management of electronic resources. Finally, in Chapter 11, we described some of the possible future directions that electronic resources may take in the future.

Sheri V. T. Ross and Sarah W. Sutton

Chapter 1
Emergence and Entrenchment of Electronic Resources in Libraries

In the context of libraries and other types of information organizations, when you hear someone refer to electronic resources, that person is most likely talking about an information resource, that is, a container of information content that requires some kind of computer mediation in order to use the content. They are "Material (data and/or program[s]) encoded for manipulation by a computerized device. This material may require the use of a peripheral directly connected to a computerized device (e.g., CD-ROM drive) or a connection to a computer network (e.g., the Internet)" (AACR and American Library 2002, sec. Glossary). This very broad term encompasses electronic books, electronic journals, digital audio files, digital video files, electronic indexes, and databases. In libraries, then, it refers to information content in a variety of electronic formats that is obtained for use by library customers. It does not generally encompass electronic (e.g., computerized) library systems like the online public access catalog (OPAC), discovery tools, integrated library systems, and so on, which are used by library staff to purchase, track, organize, and otherwise manipulate information content managed by the library. Although there will be some coverage of freely available electronic resources, the focus of this book is on fee-based, licensed electronic resources in libraries and other information institutions.

EMERGENCE OF ELECTRONIC RESOURCES IN LIBRARIES

Electronic library systems have been in use in libraries for decades. Hawthorne (2008) presents an excellent review of the early history of electronic resources in libraries from the first use of machine-readable cataloging in the 1960s to the digitization and delivery of journal indexes and bibliographic databases via CD-ROMs in the 1980s to the surge of content available via the Internet in the 1990s and 2000s.

While academic libraries have always been a primary market for licensed electronic resources, this has begun to change. Public and school libraries are responding to their customers' demand for eBooks, audio books, and other online content. In order to help them meet this demand, groups of libraries called consortia form for the purpose of sharing electronic resource costs, management, and sometimes delivery to customers. All types of libraries have become involved in consortial purchasing, which often occurs at the state library level.

Technology and rapid changes have become almost ubiquitous. eBook readers emerged as an exciting new technology in the 2000s, but until the quality of the reading experience improved, they gained little traction with the public. In 2015, the reading public has a wide variety of hardware and software for reading eBooks from which to choose. Half of all Americans owned an eBook reader or tablet computer in 2013, and they are reading eBooks on personal computers and mobile phones (Zickuhr and Rainie 2014). This created a demand that libraries lend eBooks, and libraries responded. Not only do libraries lend eBooks as well as eBook readers, but they also provide access to e-journal content, and they stream audio and video content.

Customer demand for electronic resources in libraries also resulted in the rapid and widespread adoption of demand-driven acquisition, a model for the purchase of electronic content based on customer demand. Demand-driven acquisition is not a new model per se; for example, librarians have been making purchase decisions based on interlibrary loan requests for years. What is new is the ability for a library to load a collection of eBooks into its online catalog and set a threshold number of views, checkouts, and so on, that, when reached, triggers an automatic purchase of the eBook for the library's collection. Until the threshold point is reached, the library does not acquire (or license) the book.

Rapid advances in technology also make it not just possible but easy to create and share new content via the web. The exponential growth of available electronic content makes it vital that information providers (publishers, libraries, etc.) not only deliver information but also provide the means for customers to find the right information for their purpose. This is another case not of a need to invent something brand new but of a need to allow and seek ways to promote the evolution of current practice to suit new conditions. The principles and values that underlie the practice of librarianship do not change, but the way librarians and other information providers put those principles and values into practice must change.

One change that might be attributed to the evolution of information organization and delivery is the slow but significant shift toward adding value to the tools libraries provide their customers for finding electronic resources. The first evidence of this appeared in the late 1990s and early 2000s as publishers and vendors began to develop and sell and librarians began in earnest to purchase electronic indexes (databases), which were searchable by the library customer. These evolved quickly to include value-added features like the ability to create an account in which to save search results, the ability to export bibliographic information, the ability to create a personal profile (similar to a vitae), the ability to link from an index record in one database to the full text of the article represented by that record in another database, the ability to search multiple databases with a single search, the ability to include the library catalog in a multi-database search, and the hope that soon customers will be able to retrieve library catalog results from a search of the open web.

One of the more significant results of recent technological advances is the emergence of social media. Social media have had a substantial impact on scholarly communication. Scholarly communication is

> The system through which research and other scholarly writings are created, evaluated for quality, disseminated to the scholarly community, and preserved for future use. The system includes both formal means of communication, such as publication in peer-reviewed journals, and informal channels, such as electronic listservs. (Association of Research Libraries 2015)

While scholars continue to expect that libraries will subscribe to and preserve the (mostly electronic) journals that are the traditional venues in which they communicate the results of their efforts, scholars are increasingly looking to libraries also for other services vital to the advancement of knowledge. For example, as information policy increasingly requires scholars to make the results of their work freely available to the public, librarians not only are taking part in the development of such policies, but also have developed digital institutional repositories for the preservation and dissemination of scholars' work.

Advantages of Electronic Resources to Librarians and Library Customers

Electronic resources offer a variety of advantages over print and other physical resources. One very obvious advantage is that library customers may have 24-hours-a-day, 7-days-a-week access to library electronic resources via a library's web page. Customers have instant access to library resources without the need to physically visit the library. Like books and other physical library materials, use of library electronic resources is free to library customers. But beyond these, there is a less visible, and more recently developed, advantage to electronic resources for library customers: interlinking in order to enhance the discovery of useful content. Interlinking is the capability of one electronic resource, for instance, an abstract and index (A&I) database, to link directly from a bibliographic record retrieved as a result of a search of the A&I database to the full text of the resource described in that record if it exists in another database licensed by the library. The recent advent of web-scale discovery systems provides another advantage for librarians: the need to manage a single knowledge-base.

Disadvantages of Electronic Resources to Librarians and Library Customers

Electronic resources also come with some disadvantages for librarians and library customers many of which boil down to additional complexity. For example, electronic resources are usually subscribed to by a library rather than being purchased outright so they represent an ongoing financial commitment that must be tracked, evaluated, and planned for in the budget. These activities also take staff time to complete.

Because they are more often subscribed to, which is often referred to as being licensed, electronic resources continue to belong to their publisher or creator. When the library ceases its license to use an electronic resource, their customers no longer have access to that resource. This is in contrast to a book or DVD that the library owns and can do with as it pleases (within the constraints of copyright law about which more will be discussed in Chapter 4) including continuing to lend it to customers.

The fact that the rights to copy and distribute resources are licensed to the library by a content provider means that librarians often face constraints on their customers' use of their electronic resources, constraints that may be in addition to those expressed by copyright laws. These constraints are usually agreed upon by both the licensor of the electronic resource and the subscribing library in a contract that is negotiated at the time the subscription is initiated, and that is open to renegotiation when the subscription is renewed. This process is called license negotiation or simply licensing.

Licensing, relinquishing ownership of resources, and ongoing financial commitments represent disadvantages to libraries in that librarians have, prior to the emergence of electronic resources, not had to spend limited resources to accomplish. Nevertheless, libraries are likely to continue to have information available to customers via electronic resources because demand for them is so high.

Working with Electronic Resources: Who Is Responsible?

The question of who among library staff should have responsibility for acquiring, organizing, maintaining, preserving, evaluating, and providing access to electronic resources in a library's collection is one that has evolved as the proportion of libraries' collections that are made available in electronic formats has increased. The evolution of the position of electronic resource librarians is one that in some ways parallels the growth of electronic resources in library collections, particularly in academic libraries.

Some of the first digital content that academic libraries began to collect were A&I databases and electronic versions of print journals. In some libraries it was a natural fit for serials librarians, those librarians who acquire and organize the print periodicals, to begin working with their electronic counterparts. In other libraries, however, the librarians using the resources seemed a better fit for managing them. Since this relatively new medium presented many challenges associated with their use, such as evaluating interface accessibility and usability, troubleshooting access issues, educating end users regarding the most efficient and effective means of retrieval, among other things, librarians in the traditional reference role took on the responsibility. In some cases, systems librarians have primary responsibility for electronic resources since the ongoing management and access required a higher level of comfort with technology than many librarians had at the time. In many larger institutions a team of professionals often share the work without designating a particular librarian as the electronic resource librarian; at least, that was the case in the early years.

As electronic journals became more prevalent, publishers began packaging them into collections and providing searchable databases. Third-party content providers also began offering packages of content, often based on subject area or discipline. Not only did the number of available resources proliferate, so did the systems and services to improve their discovery and access. As a consequence, workflows and professional responsibilities in academic libraries began to change. No library is the same in how it divides and organizes work among its personnel. This depends on the type of library, its overarching organizational structure, the size of its collection and user base, and its tradition of "how things are done around here."

In small libraries, it was, and still is, possible for a single professional librarian to retain responsibility for all aspects of managing electronic resources. In larger libraries, the sheer volume of materials collected in electronic formats requires the attention of multiple professional librarians. In such situations, it is common for each librarian to have responsibility for only one or two areas of the workflow or processes for evaluating, acquiring, organizing, providing access, and preserving to electronic resources in a library's collection. It was the burgeoning of the position of electronic resource librarian, the evolution of a new specialization in librarianship, which created the need to define the competencies required for such work.

A publisher's collection usually consists of items produced by a single publisher, whereas an aggregator's collection (an aggregation) usually consists of items produced by multiple publishers. An aggregation has some characteristics in common other than being published by the same entity, for instance, a subject discipline. Content provider is a term used to describe any organization that licenses electronic content to libraries.

CORE COMPETENCIES FOR THE ELECTRONIC RESOURCES LIBRARIAN

As there is with many librarian specializations, there is specialized knowledge beyond that which is core to librarianship in general, that is necessary for work with electronic resources (American Library Association 2009). Developed during 2011–2012, the *Core Competencies for Electronic Resources Librarians* (NASIG 2013) sets out a list of competences necessary for managing electronic resources in information organizations like libraries. "They are intentionally broad in scope in order to encompass work with electronic resources (ER) throughout the ER life cycle. . .[and] are intended to be used in combination with the American Library Association's Core Competences of Librarianship and, in most cases, to build on them" (NASIG 2013, 1). They are based in research conducted using job descriptions and job ads for electronic resource librarians, both of which are traditional sources of information about job responsibilities and the knowledge, skills, and experience necessary for professional success (NASIG 2013; Sutton 2011). The *Core Competencies for Electronic Resources Librarians* consist of seven areas of focus:

- Life cycle of electronic resources
- Technology
- Research and assessment
- Effective communication
- Supervising and management
- Trends and professional development
- Personal qualities (NASIG 2013)

A brief review of the core competencies is included here. The rest of this book will elucidate the competencies in the context of the stages in the life cycle of electronic resources.

Life Cycle of Electronic Resources

The advent of e-resources in libraries in the late 1990s and early 2000s created the need to reinvent workflows (Hawthorne 2008). The Digital Library Federation (DLF) made an attempt to visualize the workflows as shown in Figure 1.1. The DLF's illustration captures the increasingly complex workflows that libraries faced. But the iterative nature of the processes

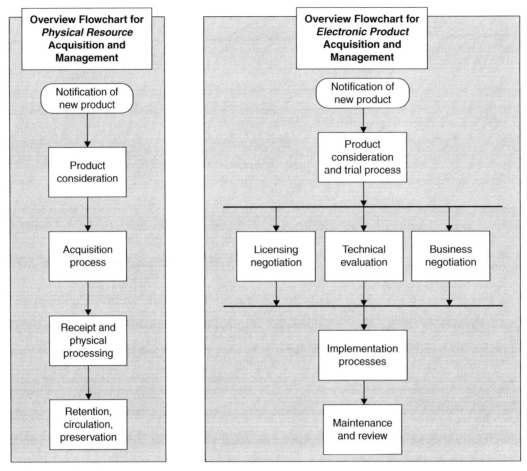

Figure 1.1 Comparison of the acquisition and management for physical and electronic resources (Jewell et al. 2004).

is best illustrated by Pesch (2011) in Figure 1.2. It is the influence of both the seriality of electronic resources and the format that makes the life cycle of electronic resources substantially more cyclical than that of physical resources, particularly books.

A serial is

> A resource issued in successive parts, usually having numbering, that has no predetermined conclusion (e.g., a periodical, a monographic series, a newspaper). Includes resources that exhibit characteristics of serials, such as successive issues, numbering, and frequency, but whose duration is limited (e.g., newsletters of events). (Joint Steering Committee for Development of RDA and American Library Association 2010, sec. Glossary)

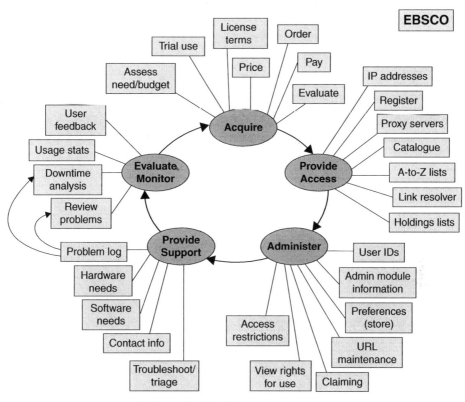

Figure 1.2 E-resources life cycle for libraries.

Because, like serials, most electronic resources are licensed (the detail of which will be covered in Chapter 3), the work of managing them is spread across their lifetime rather than being substantially greater at the initial purchase. Generally, the licensing and acquisition of an electronic resource begins the cycle. Provisions are then made to provide access to the resource to customers, usually via the library's web pages. Administration of an electronic resource includes customizing the new resource for the library's customers (adding the library's logo to the resource, setting the entry point, choosing a default search mechanism, etc.); creating links to items in the new resource from existing electronic resources, the catalog, and perhaps, an A-to-Z list of electronic resources; registering the library's IP (Internet Protocol) addresses with the electronic resource vendor; and educating library staff and customers about any restrictions on the use of the content of the resource (e.g., using content from the resource to fulfill interlibrary loan requests).

These activities are generally not one-time activities but rather must be checked and, if necessary, revised. Providing support for and troubleshooting errors are an important phase of the life cycle of an electronic resource, one that is ongoing throughout the license period. Along with maintenance, evaluation and assessment of an electronic resource is also generally ongoing. Like they do with most of their circulating resources, libraries usually measure how often an electronic resource is used by a customer, if for no other reason than to justify continuing to license it. Unlike physical library resources, electronic resources present some unique challenges to measuring their use, which will be covered in more depth in Chapter 8. The end of the cycle, if there can be said to be one, occurs annually at subscription renewal time. It is at this point that the decision is made whether or not to continue the subscription to an electronic resource for another year.

Technology

Work with electronic resources requires a depth of technological knowledge that is greater than that required of librarians working in other specialties (NASIG 2013). It does not require knowledge of or experience with computer programming (although such would certainly be useful). There are three areas of technological expertise that are necessary for work with electronic resources: hardware and software used to acquire, maintain, and assess electronic resources; standards applied to those activities; and, most important, the ability to learn to identify, implement, and maintain new technology.

Many newcomers to the management of electronic resources are intimidated by the technological knowledge and skills it requires; many professional librarian educational (MLS) programs either do not emphasize them or do not cover them at all. What newcomers often fail to recognize is that professional librarian educational programs do emphasize learning to learn. Employers of electronic resource librarians rarely expect new hires to have all of the technological competences they will need to fulfill their responsibilities. Even if they did, the rate of technological advance would shortly render them useless. What employers of librarians with electronic resources responsibilities seek and what professional librarian educational programs instill in graduates is the capability not only to keep up with rapid change, but also to recognize and learn about new technologies (hardware, software, standards, protocols, markup languages, etc.) with the potential to improve customer access to electronic resources.

Research and Assessment

Given the need to continually monitor, evaluate, and assess them, it should not be a surprise that work with electronic resources also requires substantial understanding of the research process and tools for evaluation and assessment. Electronic resources generate a tremendous amount of data, some of which is collected by the content provider from whom the librarians obtain their subscription and provide to the library; some of which is obtained for the library through third parties (e.g., organizations that collect alternative metrics such as mentions in social media or news media); and some of which is collected by the library itself. Those who work with electronic resources are usually also expected to "collect, analyze, manipulate, and provide meaningful interpretation of data using relational databases, spreadsheet and word processing programs, and other online tools" (NASIG 2013, 5). Analysis and manipulation of these data assumes knowledge of and the ability to apply both quantitative and qualitative research methods.

Effective Communication

The ability to communicate the results of data analysis is one of several forms of effective communication expected of those who work with electronic resources. Others types of communication regularly required are instruction, demonstration, persuasion, and collaboration. With regard to electronic resources, librarians should be skilled at communicating "with a broad range of internal and external audiences: users, colleagues and staff, subscription agents, and content providers; the [electronic resource librarian] must be able to tailor the message(s) to the circumstances and to the audience, as needed" (NASIG 2013, 6). It is the ability to communicate clearly to a wide range of constituents that sets the bar for communication skills in this professional specialization, from "synthesizing easy to understand summaries of complex and ambiguous phenomena" (NASIG 2013, 6) to technologically inexperienced customers at one end of the spectrum, to knowledgeably and professionally using specific terminology "to frame situations according to others' perspectives to recruit assistance with troubleshooting from content providers, agents, consortium partners, IT support" (NASIG 2013, 6) at the other end.

Supervising and Management

In typical library periodicals, acquisitions, cataloging, and other technical services workflows, non-degreed paraprofessionals are responsible for the basic routine processing of resources, while professionals, that is, degreed librarians, often supervisors, completed nonroutine processing. For example, paraprofessionals complete copy cataloging by literally copying catalog records from an external source into the library's local catalog, while professionals created new catalog records from scratch. In the early days of electronic resources in libraries, electronic resources were considered nonroutine and thus professionals managed them, often supervising paraprofessionals who performed more routine tasks. For instance, professionals negotiate contracts for electronic resources, while paraprofessionals enter contract terms into the library's local repository for such information. Thus, the role of electronic resource librarian naturally evolved as one that more often than not included supervisory and managerial responsibilities.

But as should be becoming clear, the supervisory and managerial responsibilities of an electronic resource librarian vary from those in other professional specialties. For one thing, electronic resources are a relatively new form of resource with consequent new requirements for processing. Supervisors and managers must therefore "evaluate existing procedures and workflows, revising or replacing them as needed to maximize efficiency and job performance" (NASIG 2013, 6). Their newness also creates a need for supervisory professionals to conduct staff training. But more impactful than either of these is the rapidity with which technology and therefore workflows, processes, and, of course, the resources themselves change. It often falls to the electronic resource librarian to lead both internal and external library stakeholders through increased and increasing complexity of the resources themselves, along with their constant change and ambiguity.

Trends and Development

Because of the constant change and complexity, it is necessary for those working with electronic resources in libraries to have a strong commitment to maintaining and developing their knowledge of this broad field. Current topics worth attention include scholarly communication; licensing; copyright, privacy, and other relevant legal issues; technology and related technology policies, standards, and tools; and trends and developments in the discipline of information organization. Sources of information about these and other trending topics currently include continuing education, professional conferences, webinars, the related professional literature, blogs, listservs, and social media (NASIG 2013). But these sources change as quickly as does everything else in this professional specialization, so those charged with working with electronic resources would do well to pay attention not only to changes in the topics being discussed in these sources but also to changes in the sources themselves.

Personal Qualities

It may seem slightly odd that the final section of the NASIG *Core Competencies for Electronic Resources Librarians* describes personal qualities, the possession and development of which, may benefit someone working with electronic resources in libraries. The inclusion of this section stems from evidence revealed in the research upon which the *Core Competencies for Electronic Resources Librarians* are based, specifically, the qualifications described in job advertisements for electronic resource librarians. Of job advertisements for electronic resource librarians between 2005 and 2009, 35 percent sought candidates who had a strong "customer service orientation," 34 percent sought candidates with strong "organizational skills," and 32 percent sought candidates who were flexible in the face of change (Sutton 2011, 215). All three of these categories were among the 20 qualifications most often mentioned in job ads. Thus, although they are not often overtly taught, employers clearly place a high value on these personal characteristics.

Final Words on Competencies

Among the responses to NASIG's *Core Competencies for Electronic Resources Librarians*, one of the strongest is that it would be nearly impossible for a single person to possess all of the competences it describes (Sutton 2014). In the introduction to the document, the Task Force states that

The competencies required for ERL positions vary greatly based on type of institution in which the work is done and on the workflows within the organization. For example, an ERL in a small academic library might be responsible for the entire life cycle of electronic resources in that institution, while in a large research library, an ERL might be responsible for ER acquisitions alone, while others are responsible for access, administration, support, and evaluation. (NASIG 2013, 1)

Furthermore, the uses to which the *Core Competencies for Electronic Resources Librarians* have been put since their publication suggest that libraries are using them to develop programs for staff training (Baggett 2015; Erb 2015), to reorganize workflows (Chamberlain and Reece 2013; Erb 2015), as often if not more often than they are as a checklist of knowledge, skills, and abilities to be possessed by a single person. Indeed, those who are new to electronic resources should bear in mind that "expertise is never fully achieved, and competence is always a work in progress" (Sullenger et al. 2015, sec. Abstract).

REFERENCES

AACR, Joint Steering Committee for Revision of, and Association American Library. 2002. *Anglo-American Cataloguing Rules*. Ottawa; Chicago: Canadian Library Association; American Library Association.

American Library Association. 2009. "ALA's Core Competencies of Librarianship." Chicago, IL: American Library Association Learning Round Table. Retrieved from http://wikis.ala.org/professionaltips/index.php/Competencies.

American National Standards Institute. 2015. "About Page." New York: American National Standards Institute. Retrieved from http://www.ansi.org/about_ansi/overview/overview.aspx?menuid=1.

Association of Research Libraries. 2015. "Scholarly Communication." *Association of Research Libraries*. Accessed June 7. Retrieved from http://www.arl.org/focus-areas/scholarly-communication#.VXSLU2C5ykQ.

Baggett, Stacy B. 2015. "Deconstructing the Core Competencies to Build the Digital Future." Poster presentation presented at the NASIG 30th Annual Conference, Washington, DC, May 28.

Chamberlain, Clint, and Derek Reece. 2013. "Library Reorganization, Chaos, and Using the Core Competencies as a Guide." Presented at the NASIG 2013 Annual Conference, Buffalo, New York, June 8.

Erb, Rachel A. 2015. "The Impact of Reorganization of Staff Using the Core Competencies as a Framework for Staff Training and Development." *The Serials Librarian* 68 (1–4): 92–105. doi:10.1080/0361526X.2015.1017417.

Hawthorne, Dalene. 2008. "History of Electronic Resources." In *Electronic Resource Management in Libraries: Research and Practice*, edited by Holly Yu and Schott Breivold. Hershey, PA: Information Science Reference.

Jewell, T., et al. 2004. "Report of the DLF ERM Initiative." Washington, DC: Digital Library Federation.

Joint Steering Committee for Development of RDA, and American Library Association. 2010. *Resource Description and Access: RDA*. Chicago, IL: American Library Association.

NASIG. 2013. "NASIG Core Competencies for Electronic Resources Librarians." Retrieved from http://www.nasig.org/uploaded_files/92/files/CoreComp/CompetenciesforERLibrarians_final_ver_2013-7-22.pdf.

Pesch, Oliver. 2011. "E-Resource Standards You Should Know About." *The Serials Librarian* 61 (2): 215–30. doi:10.1080/0361526X.2011.591043.

Sullenger, Paula, Shade Aladebumoye, Nadine Ellero, and Susan Wishnetsky. 2015. "Core Competencies to the Rescue: Taking Stock and Protecting Institutional Knowledge." *The Serials Librarian* 68 (1–4): 223–29. doi:10.1080/0361526X.2015.1017708.

Sutton, Sarah. 2011. *Identifying Core Competencies for Electronic Resources Librarians in the Twenty-First Century Library*. Denton, TX: Texas Woman's University.

Sutton, Sarah. 2014. "Update on and Discussion of the Core Competencies for Electronic Resources Librarians." Presented at the American Library Association Midwinter Meeting, Philadelphia, PA, January 25. http://listserv.nasig.org/scripts/wa-NASIG.exe?A0=SERIALST.

Zickuhr, Kathryn, and Lee Rainie. 2014. "E-Reading Rises as Device Ownership Jumps." *Pew Research Center's Internet & American Life Project*. Retrieved from http://www.pewinternet.org/2014/01/16/e-reading-rises-as-device-ownership-jumps/.

Chapter 2
The Information Environment

The information environment is a complex ever-changing organism, particularly as the Internet and digital content have connected content creators and content consumers around the globe. It has spurred new social science models, changes in policy and law, and cultures of creativity and sharing. The business facet of the information environment comprises developments in the information industry, which is a widely encompassing sector. It includes not only content creation and distribution, but also areas such as content management, search analytics, social media, and big data. While electronic resource librarians may wish to become familiar with these and other related fields, they will likely want to focus their attention on the supply chain of digital content, which includes publishing, aggregating, and the distribution and delivery of content.

The organizations involved in the information supply chain interact and overlap in ways that are nicely understood through basic microeconomic concepts. Publishers, vendors, systems providers, and librarians all work together to ensure that the appropriate end user has the efficient and effective access to digital content as possible. This is accomplished through an array of collaborative endeavors that electronic resource librarians should understand and in which they should participate, if possible. Participation may include serving on a product advisory board or participating in a pricing model focus group. More formally, collaborative work among these parties is mediated through the standards development process, which is covered in Chapter 3.

DIGITAL CONTENT PROVIDERS

When librarians refer to digital content providers, they usually mean those organizations that provide content to libraries. That is, those organizations the librarian deals with directly, such as a database vendor who aggregates content and delivers it through a proprietary platform, or a book vendor who offers eBooks through an approval plan, or an open-access digital repository that exposes its metadata for harvesting into the library's discovery index. Several publishers offer their own delivery platform and deal directly with libraries as well. However, many publishers, particularly smaller and not-for-profit organization, have opted to license their content to aggregators, which then provide the distribution and delivery to libraries. Often, librarians will license or purchase materials through a third party, like a consortium, which are not considered content providers in the usual sense.

> A content delivery platform in this context refers to the software that a vendor uses to provide content through the World Wide Web. The platform includes a user-friendly interface with search and retrieval tools, as well as tools for consuming the content, such as a reading pane or a link to a downloadable file.

Early Days of Digital Content

A 2005 article called "Online before the Internet" in *Information Today* lays out the early history of the online information environment. This is a very interesting recounting of two early online systems, DIALOG and ORBIT, which both began as large government contractor companies. The article is a transcription of a joint interview with the founders of these two companies, Roger Summit and Carlos Cuadra, respectively, as they attempt to recall the milestones of their careers and the life of their respective businesses. Other interviews include Richard (Dick) Giering, who from 1967 to 1978 was instrumental in developing the "underlying basic technology" that ultimately led to the creation of Lexis Nexis. Jan Egeland, one of the founders of Bibliographic Retrieval Services, a commercial system that grew out of the Biomedical Communication Network, and Melvin S. Day, often mentioned by the pioneers in this series as a champion and facilitator of new technologies that appeared throughout the 1960s and 1970s. Mr. Day began his government information career in 1946 at the U.S. Atomic Energy Commission. As documents from the Manhattan Project were declassified, he was responsible for their indexing, creating what later was known as Nuclear Science Abstracts.

DIALOG is still available for use today and is owned by ProQuest, which acquired it from Thomson Reuters in 2008, which acquired it from Market Analysis Information Databases (MAID) in 2000, which acquired it from Knight-Ridder in 1998, which acquired it from Lockheed in 1981.

In these early examples, the government was largely responsible for the creation of the content for these databases. The content delivery platforms were basic command line search and retrieval tools. They were simple, yet provided powerful search functionality that required specialized expertise to be used effectively and efficiently. When products like Dialog and Lexis became commercially available, librarians would dial up and connect directly to the database through the telephone line network. Fees for use were based on the number of searches performed, amount of time searching, the number of citations retrieved, or some combination of these. Hence, searching expertise was an important asset in the early online environment. Today's database environment is largely an all-you-can-read affair. Searching has become simplified, and an overabundance of retrieved citations is often the norm.

Content Publishers

While government publishing is still strong, it is the private sector that has been driving innovation in scholarly publishing. The number of publishers and publishing venues continues to grow, and content delivery systems have evolved to meet the tastes of modern information consumers. Publishers are those individuals and their organizations that produce and ensure the dissemination of information or creative works. They will copyedit, mediate the processes of peer review, add graphic elements, format for distribution, and market the work.

The process of publishing, or making available to the public, ensures that the author of a work will be endowed with the appropriate copyrights. In the scholarly communication environment, often, an author will contract some or all of these copyrights with a journal publisher in exchange for the value added through the publishing process. This once was a straightforward transaction for authors; however, librarians, among others, have raised awareness around alternate contracting possibilities, such as open-access publishing, which is discussed later.

Publishers come in many shapes and sizes. According to the Association of American Publishers, "virtually all publishers lead the full continuum of investment in ideas, development, production, curation, editing, marketing, copyright protection and delivery required to convert unique visions to reality" (Association of American Publishers 2015). And they do so on every media platform and in every format available now and in the future. More than 300 organizations comprise their membership. These span all "categories of publishing and represent the major commercial, educational and professional companies as well as independents, non-profits, university presses and scholarly societies" (Association of American Publishers 2015). There is a Trade Division, School Division, Higher Education Division, and the Professional and Scholarly Publishing Division.

From the perspective of the electronic resource librarian, publishers might be divided into four categories: for-profit publishers, not-for-profit publishers, open-access publishing in which the author pays for the cost of publication, and open-access publishing in which publication costs are covered by organizations such as professional associations or university libraries. The first two of these four categories are largely continuations of publishing models from the print era. These are publishers of books, periodicals, newspapers, and multimedia content with long-established processes for publication and distribution. While there was radical change in the technological aspects of publishing and distribution, the ways in which digital content was perceived as distinct from print was slow to change; the revolutionary possibilities went unacknowledged by traditional publishers.

Recognizing the potential for timelier and more widespread distribution of digital content, authors, librarians, and other interested parties have supported the growth of open-access publishing. Open access will be addressed in greater detail in Chapter 10. For now, recognize that the purpose is to remove barriers of access to the end user, legal and financial. Open-access publications allow the reader to, at the very least, read the content free of charge. Figures 2.1 and 2.2 illustrate the differences between the proprietary model of scholarly publishing and the open-access model of scholarly publishing.

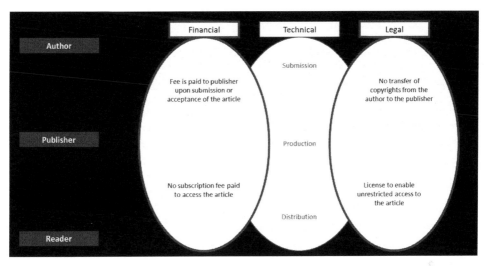

Figure 2.1 Proprietary model of scholarly publishing.

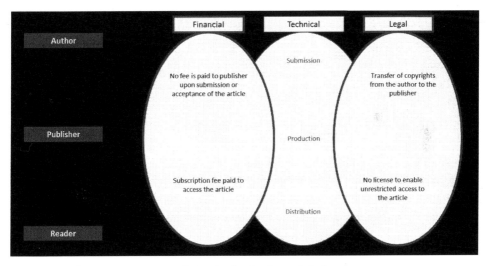

Figure 2.2 Open-access model of scholarly publishing.

There are two primary means of open-access publishing. One way is to publish in an open-access journal. This is sometimes referred to as the gold road to open access. In this model, authors or their institutions may cover the cost of publication and distribution by paying a fee to the open-access journal or authors may choose to submit their work to an open-access journal run by volunteers and sponsored by an interested organization. In the second open-access model, sometimes called the green road to open access, authors make their work available through self-publishing on their website, an institutional repository, or a discipline-based repository.

> An institutional repository (IR) is a digital archive of an institution's intellectual output. They are commonly found in colleges and universities. Librarians are often involved with the development and management of institutional repositories because they bring expertise in the areas of collecting, organizing, preserving, and disseminating digital content.

Content Vendors

Database vendors are the organizational entities with whom the electronic resource librarian will most often interact. Vendors are also known as aggregators and content providers. Before the advent of widespread digital content, vendors served as the intermediaries between publishers and libraries. A vendor might have represented dozens of publishing interests with selections of thousands of publications. They offered librarians a one-stop shopping experience; this was especially useful for the acquisition of serial publications. Vendors serve this same function in the era of digital content. However, today, they not only aggregate publications from multiple publishers, but also market, index, and disseminate them. Vendors offer sophisticated platforms for their databases of content and are often more recognizable as a brand to the end user than titles of the publications contained within.

Database vendors can be small specialized organizations or very large conglomerates. The larger organizations tend to have a higher capacity for product development and drive innovation in the areas of search and retrieval, content usability and cross-referencing, and value-add components that improves the end-user experience. These platform innovations are often proprietary and are offered to libraries at a premium. At the same time, these large database vendors have reached an economy of scale that allows them to earn considerable profit once production costs are covered. In this way, pricing can often be as reasonable as those offered by smaller database providers that may have a smaller subscription base and have difficulty reaching a break-even point. Of course, the price of the product is only one factor in the equation. If a product is unique, without comparable substitutes, offered only by one vendor, and required by the library's user community, subscription prices will likely be difficult to negotiate.

Electronic resource librarians interact with database vendors and their products on a daily basis. They will typically be tasked with researching available products in a given discipline or in a certain format and report back to collection development librarians. The electronic resource librarian will need to assess usage of the products and report back to decision makers regarding the perceived value of the products based on their use by the user community. The electronic resource librarian will also need to troubleshoot interruptions in content access. These databases interoperate with several other software products managed by the library that, working together, provide effective search functionality and seamlessly deliver requested content to the library user. If there is an interruption in this larger system of interrelated software, the electronic resource librarian will need to discover where the problem lies. In many cases, this requires communication with a vendor's customer service department.

The interrelated software systems mentioned in the previous paragraph are often offered through the same organizations that supply libraries with digital content. For the sake of disambiguation, however, these vendors will be referred to here as systems vendors. Systems vendors offer various software systems that work together to provide a seamless search and retrieval tool across multiple databases and platforms. These include authentication software, knowledge base software, open-URL linking software, discovery layer software, statistical reporting software, and software for the management of administrative metadata. All of these systems will be covered in future chapters. Ideally, these systems are interoperable not only with each other, but also with the library's legacy integrated library system. Systems are in development, which attempt to integrate all library activity from cataloging, to digital content delivery to the circulation of print books.

These products are often offered together as a package by a given systems vendor. Some systems vendors come from the stock of organizations that initially developed integrated library management systems. They are also offered by those same organizations that provide content databases and their platforms. The software components, often referred to as modules, have distinct functions and are designed according to industry standards. In theory, a module from one service provider should be interoperable with a module from a different service provider. The systems may be easier to administer and troubleshoot if acquired as a package from a single source. This may also reap a benefit in terms of cost. However, determining which modules to acquire from a given provider is often dependent upon legacy systems, consortial arrangements, and the availability of open-source alternatives, among other factors.

DIGITAL CONTENT SUPPLY CHAIN

The evolution of content from print to primarily digital caused a rethinking of the relationship between libraries, publishers, and vendors. Academic librarians, in particular, began to pay more attention to the scholarly publication system. It is often mentioned that the price increases of academic journal subscriptions outpaced the rate of inflation. The inability to keep the acquisitions budget at pace led to a reaction by librarians who felt they were being victimized by publishers. Unfortunately, this caused a rift in the long-standing relationship between the content industry and librarians, which is still mending. As service-oriented professionals often employed in not-for-profit organizations, librarians typically haven't concerned themselves with the dynamics of the competitive marketplace from which they acquire many of their products. This has become a necessary component of the knowledge base of electronic resource librarians. To enter into effective relationships with publishers, database vendors, and service providers, electronic resource librarians should be aware of and understand the microeconomic environment in which they operate.

Dynamics of a Competitive Marketplace

Microeconomics is the study of how individuals, households, and businesses make economic decisions in a competitive marketplace. It relies heavily on the theory of supply and demand. Demand for a product or service refers to the quantity that buyers are willing and able to pay at a given price. Supply of a product or service refers to the quantity that sellers are willing and able to produce at a given price. If supply and demand are plotted on a graph, they create two curves that intersect at a point of equilibrium. Theoretically, this is the optimum price for a product or service and will satisfy both the buyer and the seller. If there is too much supply, there will be a surplus, and the price of the product will go down. If

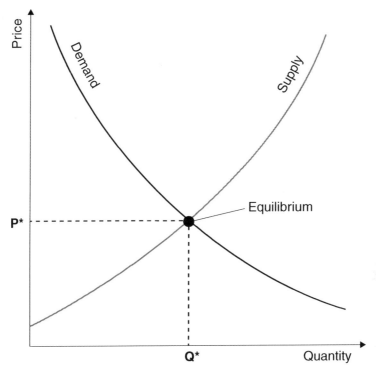

Figure 2.3 Supply and demand curve.

there is too little supply, this creates scarcity, and the price of the product will rise accordingly.

For this theory to work on the ground, it is necessary to have a competitive marketplace. Perfect competition rarely exists, but for economic optimization in a capitalist society, its tenets should be strived for. Perfect competition requires that:

- Markets for a product or service have many buyers and sellers.
- The products and services offered in a market are comparable.
- Producers/sellers face no substantial barrier to entry.
- Both buyers and sellers have perfect information to inform their decision making.

This list illustrates the type of environment librarians would like to operate in. It would be ideal to have many sellers in the marketplace; to have several comparable options for the various content, platforms, and services; to continually have new vendors entering the market with original ideas and solutions; and to have perfect information regarding the product they are considering acquiring. The perfect competition model of microeconomics is theoretical and really applicable only on a smaller scale. Today's market is international, operates in a complex legal environment, and is controlled by a handful of powerful players.

One factor that reduces the possibility of perfect competition is the status granted to corporations. Corporations, particularly for-profit corporations, are often the producers and sellers of content, platforms, and services. They have many advantages over the unincorporated, often the buyer. While they are considered by law to be like natural persons, often called fictional persons or legal persons, they enjoy economic and legal benefits that the unincorporated do not.

- Separation of management and shareholders.
- Shareholders represented by a board of directors.
- Affords limited liability to its shareholders.
- Unlimited life span, but can be easily dissolved if a situation warrants.

In an economic environment saturated with corporations, it is clear why perfect competition cannot exist. As a producer or seller, a corporate entity has a distinct advantage over a noncorporate entity. There is an unequal amount of investment. The limited liability afforded to shareholders of corporations has the effect of shielding them from possible negative consequences of bad decision making. For instance, a product or service may have been misrepresented to buyers creating a situation where there was less than perfect information for the buyer. If the corporation refuses to remedy any defect that was misrepresented, the buyers may sue, but only the corporation, not the shareholders, would be accountable for losses.

Market Power

Some corporate power is so concentrated that oligopolies or monopolies exist. This happens when only one or a few sellers have market power. That is, they are able to effectively control the entry of others into the market. As opposed to the perfect competition model where sellers are considered "price takers," in this situation, the monopolists or oligopolists are "price makers." They are able to maximize profits by producing fewer goods and selling them at higher prices.

Three categories of monopoly are natural, government granted, and coercive. The first of these, natural monopoly, occurs in an industry where it is more cost effective for the production to be carried out by a single firm, rather than having firms compete. This situation occurs most often when initial capital costs are prohibitively high, such as setting up an electric grid. This presents a barrier to entry to all but the first and/or wealthiest market entrant. A very large market would be necessary for the firm to be able to recoup its investment and maintain the capital infrastructure.

The second is the government granted. Sometimes, it is necessary for governments to provide firms with an incentive to make the initial capital investment, particularly if the product or services are deemed to be essential for the public good. Municipalities, for instance, will often grant limited-term monopolies for a cable provider in exchange for the building

"I Like a Little Competition"—J. P. Morgan

Figure 2.4 "I Like a Little Competition" by Art Young (1913).

and maintenance of the infrastructure. Another type of government-granted monopoly can be seen in the various rights accorded to creators of intellectual property, such as copyrights or patents.

While monopolies in and of themselves are not illegal, there are practices of coercive monopolies that are. Practices such as preventing competitors from entering or competing in the marketplace or price fixing and underselling are illegal. The practice of merging with or acquiring other firms that may give the opportunity to take advantage of those practices is highly scrutinized by the federal government. For instance, a publishing interest may be acquired by database vendor, giving it advantages in distribution (vertical integration) and the potential to disadvantage its competitors. Or a database vendor may acquire or secure exclusive contracts with publishers of similar and competing content. This affords the advantage of securing a greater share of the potential market (horizontal integration).

As librarians, it is easy to forget that our economy is driven by profit motive. However, "free-market" dynamics have never been a secret, and corporations should be expected to behave like corporations. Fortunately, the development of innovative desirable products often increases profits; excellent customer service is necessary to maintain profits; and engendering social goodwill among its customers through initiatives like scholarships or conference underwriting also has the potential to increase profits. Electronic resource librarians interact with the greater economic environment in ways that many librarians do not. They should always check themselves and consider things from the perspective of the publisher, database vendor, or service provider before interacting with their representatives. This effort, along with the recognition that all parties play an important role in the information ecosystem, will engender more productive relationships.

ACTIVITIES

1. The *Charleston Advisor* is an excellent resource for monitoring developments in the electronic resources landscape. Look over the reviews in a recent edition and select a publisher or vendor of one of the reviewed products that you find interesting.
   a. Research the history of the organization, particularly with respect to any mergers and acquisitions.
   b. How have there been attempts by this organization to vertically or horizontally integrate?

   c. What do you believe the impact of these activities has been or will be on libraries?

2. In her work titled *Scholarship in the Digital Age* (2007), Christine Borgman notes that "the delicate balance between the roles of scholars, publishers and librarians that existed in the print world is now askew" (p. 77).

   a. What are some factors that might have led to this imbalance?

   b. Identify any structural or processual changes that she might be referring to in this quote.

   c. Brainstorm ideas that might bring order back to these relationships and strengthen the scholarly communication system.

REFERENCES

Association of American Publishers. 2015. "About Page." Washington, DC: Association of American Publishers. Retrieved from http://publishers.org/about/overview.

Bjourner, S., and Ardito S.C. "Online before the Internet: Early Pioneers Tell Their Stories." *Searcher*, June 2003. Medford, NJ: Information Today, Inc. Retrieved from http://www.infotoday.com/searcher/jun03/ardito_bjorner.shtml.

Borgman, C.L. 2007. *Scholarship in the Digital Age: Information, Infrastructure and the Internet*. Cambridge, MA: MIT Press.

Ross, S.V.T. 2006. In advanced examinations toward a Doctor of Philosophy Degree, Florida State University.

Young, A. "I Like a Little Competition." In *The Masses*, February 1913. Retrieved from http://www.marxists.org/subject/art/visual_arts/satire/young/.

FURTHER READING

Against the Grain: Linking Publishers, Vendors, and Librarians. Charleston, SC: Against the Grain, LLC.

The Charleston Advisor: Critical Reviews of Web Products for Information Professionals. Denver: The Charleston Company.

The Charleston Report: Business Insights into the Library Market. Denver: The Charleston Company.

EContent Magazine. Medford, NJ: Information Today, Inc.

Joseph, H. 2013. "The Emerging Open Access Policy Framework in the United States." Washington, DC: The Scholarly Publishing and Academic Resources Coalition (SPARC).

ONLINE Magazine. Medford, NJ: Information Today, Inc.

Chapter 3
Information Standards

Information standards are the foundation of many library systems and have helped to create an environment that is more efficient, affordable, and interoperable. Without standards, there would be no International Standard Book Number (ISBN) and no MAchine Readable Cataloging (MARC) record. The ISBN, for instance, ensures that every manifestation of a published book is assigned a unique identifier. This standard is instrumental in the efficient operation of publishers, vendors, and libraries. It allows for all copies of a particular title to be grouped together, and it enables the disambiguation of books that may have the same title. For libraries, having an ISBN attached to the manifestation of a work has provided catalogers with a way to share bibliographic records easily; the information associated with the ISBN, such as title, author, and publisher, is the same for every instance of the book and so a single catalog record may be used by every library to record their holding. Similarly, reference librarians can use the ISBN to quickly identify a work of interest in a catalog or collocate records for a work across multiple catalogs.

An efficient information environment is one that performs with maximum productivity, minimizing wasted time and resources.

An affordable information environment is one in which content and systems are exchanged by links in the supply chain at a fair market price.

An interoperable information environment is one that fosters systems and standards that promote the exchange of data and metadata within and among organizations.

Every library has a Library Management System (LMS) or Integrated Library System (ILS). These are, of course, the systems that automate all of the operations of the physical library. They have multiple modules that work together to manage everything from the acquisition process to the circulation process. Every ILS is customized to work within a particular library environment and so seems quite unique. However, the library ILS is based on standard protocols that allow metadata and data to be effectively stored, retrieved, and exchanged to accomplish the library's objectives. The most well known would be the MARC record. MARC is a protocol that computers use to exchange catalog metadata with other computers.

Most libraries today also have a suite of software services for the management of electronic resources that are likewise based on agreed-upon standards, protocols, and best practices. These are used by organizations in the information supply chain to ensure efficiency and interoperability among and between publishers, vendors, and libraries. Publishers and vendors benefit because their content and software products will be easily integrated into an existing system. Vendors, in particular, are able to focus on improving the nonstandardized aspects of their products, driving innovation and potentially new standards. Libraries benefit by being assured that digital content will be delivered in the most effective manner and that systems will effectively support the management of digital content.

Information standards are developed both in the United States and internationally. Many information standards in the United States have been developed and maintained by the National Information Standards Organization (NISO). The umbrella organization under which NISO stands is the American National Standards Institute (ANSI). ANSI is a clearing house for "norms and guidelines that directly impact businesses in nearly every sector: from acoustical devices to construction equipment, from dairy and livestock production to energy distribution, and many more" (ANSI 2015). At the international level, the International Organization for Standardization (ISO) provides guidance for standardizing products and processes at a global level, bringing efficiencies to trade and travel among other things.

Of course, other organizations and associations develop and maintain information standards for libraries as well. Standards for metadata development and exchange, for instance, emanate from many organizations such as the American Library Association, the Society of American Archivists, and the Visual Resources Association. Metadata value standards including subject heading lists and discipline-based thesauri have been developed and are promulgated by organizations such as the Library of Congress and the Getty Research Institute. Standards, norms, and best practices are produced by nearly every subfield of librarianship to guide professionals in their work. It is necessary for professional librarians to know about, understand, and use standards. This is especially true for electronic resource librarians who deal with complex systems using an array of interrelated standards. These are living documents and change over time to reflect changes in the industry they are meant to serve. Keeping apprised of standards in development or under revision should be a priority for the electronic resource librarian.

Many of the divisions of ALA have a "Standards Committee." The Association for Library Collections and Technical Services, for instance, actively promotes engagement by its members in the standards development process and works closely with NISO.

INTERNATIONAL STANDARDS

ISO is often referred to as the International Standards Organization, but is formally called in English the International Organization for Standardization. Established in 1947 and located in Geneva, Switzerland, ISO is an overarching standards body that develops and maintains guidelines for everything from social responsibility for business, to screw thread sizing, to prosthetics description. It has published more than 19,500 standards to ensure that products and systems work safely and efficiently. ISO comprises 163 member countries each of which has its own national standards body (ISO 2015a). For the most part, electronic resource librarians will be interested in the work of two committees. The first is the Technical

Committee ISO-TC46, called Information and Documentation. This technical committee or TC currently has five subcommittees or SCs:

- ISO/TC46/SC4   Technical interoperability
- ISO/TC46/SC8   Quality—Statistics and performance evaluation
- ISO/TC46/SC9   Identification and description
- ISO/TC46/SC10   Requirements for document storage and conditions for preservation
- ISO/TC46/SC11   Archives/records management (ISO 2015c)

The second committee of interest is the Joint Technical Committee, JTC1, which brings together experts in several areas of information and communications technology (ICT) to formulate standards. It addresses issues of information technology, including IT governance, user interfaces, and information security, among others. According to ISO, JTC1 has developed "very successful and relevant ICT standards in the fields of multimedia (e.g., MPEG), IC cards ("smart cards"), ICT security, database query and programming languages as well as character sets, to name just a few" (ISO 2015b). Its various subcommittees follow.

- ISO/IEC JTC1/SC2   Coded character sets
- ISO/IEC JTC1/SC6   Telecommunications and information exchange between systems
- ISO/IEC JTC1/SC7   Software and systems engineering
- ISO/IEC JTC1/SC17   Cards and personal identification
- ISO/IEC JTC1/SC22   Programming languages, their environments, and system software interfaces
- ISO/IEC JTC1/SC23   Digitally recorded media for information interchange and storage
- ISO/IEC JTC1/SC24   Computer graphics, image processing, and environmental data representation
- ISO/IEC JTC1/SC25   Interconnection of information technology equipment
- ISO/IEC JTC1/SC27   IT security techniques
- ISO/IEC JTC1/SC28   Office equipment
- ISO/IEC JTC1/SC29   Coding of audio, picture, multimedia, and hypermedia information
- ISO/IEC JTC1/SC31   Automatic identification and data capture techniques
- ISO/IEC JTC1/SC32   Data management and interchange
- ISO/IEC JTC1/SC34   Document description and processing languages
- ISO/IEC JTC1/SC35   User interfaces

- ISO/IEC JTC1/SC36   Information technology for learning, education, and training
- ISO/IEC JTC1/SC37   Biometrics
- ISO/IEC JTC1/SC38   Cloud computing and distributed platforms
- ISO/IEC JTC1/SC39   Sustainability for and by information technology
- ISO/IEC JTC1/SC40   IT Service management and IT governance (ISO 2015b)

The United States usually has representation on JTC1 and TC46 and its subcommittees. The United States is represented in the ISO through ANSI. ANSI, formed in 1916, is a national body that coordinates standards development and serves as a clearinghouse for the work of standards developing agencies in the United States. It is of course in the best interests of the United States to contribute to standards development at the international level as it increases its global competitiveness. Moreover, as a member of the World Trade Organization, which administers the Technical Barrier to Trade Agreement, the United States is bound to encourage the use of international standards rather than national or regional ones.

The International Bureau of Weights and Measures (BIPM) is the official maintenance organization for the International System of Units. Of course, the United States and the United Kingdom do not measure distance and mass like the rest of the world. We use yards and pounds, while everyone else uses meters and grams. This can be confusing when traveling. How many kilometers per hour am I driving—will I be getting a speeding ticket in the mail? How many grams of lobster are reasonable for one person to order? Just another great reason to standardize!

NATIONAL STANDARDS

Standards are used to formulate policy and regulate industry in the countries that adopt them. In the United States, the National Technology Transfer and Advancement Act of 1995 mandated that all federal agencies and departments use, wherever possible, technical standards that are developed or adopted by voluntary consensus standards bodies for their regulations. The act became Public Law 104–113 in 1916. It directs the

National Institute of Standards and Technology to coordinate with other federal agencies, as well as state, and local governments and the private sector to achieve greater reliance on voluntary standards and less on regulations developed in-house (National Institute of Standards and Technology 2015). While standards are not law, laws might mandate that standards be used. Often state and municipal laws will mandate the adherence to a code, such is the case for the National Electrical Code ANSI/NFPA 70.

Likewise, regulatory bodies themselves may depend on published standards to guide their work. For instance, the U.S. Department of Labor's Occupational Safety and Health Administration relies on "national consensus standards" to help execute its mission. They define national consensus standards as any standard or modification thereof which:

1. "has been adopted and promulgated by a nationally recognized standards-producing organization under procedures whereby it can be determined by the Secretary of Labor or by the Assistant Secretary of Labor that persons interested and affected by the scope or provisions of the standard have reached substantial agreement on its adoption,
2. was formulated in a manner which afforded an opportunity for diverse views to be considered, and has been designated as such a standard by the Secretary or the Assistant Secretary, after consultation with other appropriate Federal agencies." (OSHA 2015)

In the private sector, standards are voluntarily adopted for the purposes of interoperability with component products as well as showing goodwill to their customers and competitors. If a firm were to try to patent a process or procedure that had been widely adopted by a segment of industry, their reputation would likely suffer for what might be considered anti-competitive behavior. This actually happened during the development of the open URL standard. After years of development by several vested parties from the content provider sector and libraries, it came to light that someone had filed a patent on the technology. The repercussions of this could have meant that the content providers would have to pay a fee each time an end user clicked on the "Find it" button to retrieve an article. Of course, this cost would be passed on to libraries. However, the patent holder granted the use of the technology to the community without having to pay fees.

The universe of standards development is changing. Today, there is much more private sector involvement and a greater emphasis on international standards development. According to ANSI, a decade ago, 80 percent of all standardization activities of the European standards bodies focused on national work, with the remainder related to European and international development efforts. Today, this ratio is reversed: 80 percent of standards work is international. Due to the increasingly global marketplace, there is less momentum for developing national standards; however, a great need for national standards remains. The people of the world are diverse. A variety of languages and cultures require standards to meet the specific needs of these diverse peoples. For instance, packaging requirements may be specific to a locality, or size specifications for dwellings. Also standards for professional behavior may be considerably different from country to country.

NISO is a central location for information standards, not only for librarians, but also for publishers, and those who develop delivery platforms in the United States. Its website introduces the organization thusly:

> NISO is where content publishers, libraries, and software developers turn for information industry standards that allow them to work together. Through NISO, all of these communities are able to collaborate on mutually accepted standards. (National Information Standards Organization 2015b)

NISO was formed in 1939, when a committee was put in place by the American Standards Association to manage the newly emerging Z39 standards series. It was appropriately called Committee Z39 and was headed up by the American Library Association. In the early 1950s, leadership was transferred to the Council of Library Associations. The first Z39 standard had been put into place two years prior. Z39.1 was called Reference Data for Periodicals (NISO 2015a). NISO also sends representatives to work with ISO. In 1947, ISO TC46 on Information and Documentation was formed. NISO has been designated by ANSI as the U.S. Technical Advisory Group (TAG) Administrator for TC46. NISO voting members located in the United States make up the TAG membership and may participate in voting and commenting on proposed standards.

According to the NISO website, the scope of the work of T46 is: "standardization of practices relating to libraries, documentation and information centres, publishing, archives, records management, museum documentation, indexing and abstracting services, and information science" (NISO 2015e).

T46 currently has four working groups:

- WG 2, Coding of country names and related entities—This working group is responsible for the ISO 3166 series of standards, informally called country codes.
- WG 3, Conversion of written languages—This working group is responsible for various language transliteration and romanization standards.
- WG 4, Terminology of information and documentation—This working group is currently in hiatus.
- WG 7, Presentation of periodicals.

Electronic resource librarians should be familiar with several standards and recommended protocols (RPs) developed and maintained by NISO. While many of the older standards were put into place to facilitate efficiencies in publishing and cataloging during the print era, most of the more recent standards have emerged to handle efficiencies in the delivery and management of digital content. In particular, the work of the NISO Discovery to Delivery Topic Committee and the Business Information Topic Committee, both formed in early 2007 during an organizational restructuring, should be on the electronic resource librarian's radar. Each committee handles a portfolio of standards and recommended practices that are relevant to their directive.

The Discovery to Delivery Topic Committee brings together leaders from companies that supply content and develop systems, as well as specialists from American libraries. According to their committee description, the Discovery to Delivery Topic Committee "focuses on issues regarding the finding and distribution of information by and to users, including OpenURL, Metasearch, interface design, web services, etc." (NISO 2015c). The Business Information Topic Committee "focuses on issues regarding the management structure surrounding the acquisition, licensing, purchasing, and analysis of information. Specific areas include: license expression, online usage data, access management, performance measures and other statistics, etc." (NISO 2015d).

These standards are often technical in nature, use specialized vocabulary, and will likely not be fully comprehensible at this stage of reading of this text. These standards will be revisited in the chapters to follow in the context of their applications in practice. The following is a sampling of the NISO standards, protocols, and recommended practices that affect the management of electronic resources.

- ANSI/NISO Z39.84–2005 (R2010) Syntax for the Digital Object Identifier
- ANSI/NISO Z39.88–2004 (R2010) The OpenURL Framework for Context-Sensitive Services
- ANSI/NISO Z39.93–2014 The Standardized Usage Statistics Harvesting Initiative (SUSHI) Protocol
- ANSI/NISO Z39.96–2012 JATS: Journal Article Tag Suite
- NISO RP-7–2012, SERU: A Shared Electronic Resource Understanding
- NISO RP-9–2014, Knowledge Base and Related Tools (KBART)
- NISO RP-10–2010, Cost of Resource Exchange (CORE) Protocol
- NISO RP-14–2014, NISO SUSHI Protocol: COUNTER-SUSHI Implementation Profile
- NISO RP-16–2013, PIE-J: The Presentation & Identification of E-Journals
- NISO RP-19–2014, Open Discovery Initiative: Promoting Transparency in Discovery
- NISO RP-21–2013, Improving OpenURLs through Analytics (IOTA): Recommendations for Link Resolver Providers

Often, standards will be developed and approved simultaneously or very close in time by more than one organization. This is why the electronic resource librarian might see more than one designation for any given standard. For instance, ANSI/NISO Z39.88. This is the standard designation for the OpenURL protocol and was first approved by NISO in February 2010 and then approved by ANSI in May 2010.

PROFESSIONAL STANDARDS

In the early days of electronic resource management, The Digital Library Federation (DLF) was instrumental in identifying and articulating the systematic components for the effective and efficient management of electronic resources. In the early 2000s, the DLF published a report, "Electronic Resource Management: The Report of the DLF Initiative," which set the stage for the development of the many standards to come in this area. This was a time of acute change in libraries, and the DLF described the problem at hand as "the acquisitions and licensing processes are complex, publishers transmit this information to libraries in a variety of paper and electronic formats, and the number of licensed electronic products that libraries are collecting is increasing rapidly. Such situations tend to spawn local, ad hoc fixes; what is needed, by contrast, is an industry-wide, standardized solution. The Electronic Resources Management Initiative (ERMI), an ongoing project of the Digital Library Federation (DLF), is creating such a solution" (Digital Library Federation 2004). Refer to Figure 1.1 to review how the DLF Report compares the workflows of print and electronic resources.

This report was vital to the initial development of Electronic Resource Management Systems (ERMS). As is pointed out, librarians were spending a great deal of time and resources creating local systems to help them manage the administrative functions of electronic resource management. Commercial developers have introduced a number of products to the library market that facilitate some of these processes, but their adoption by libraries seems to be slow; the ad hoc locally grown systems seem to work just fine for now. Standards for the exchange of business information and licensing terms have been agreed on, but parties to transactions are slow to implement the new products.

Koppel (2008) notes that the DLF Report became known as the "DLF Spec" and that certain appendices were instrumental in the development of the commercial ERMS on the market today. Appendix A of the report covers the functions of an electronic resource management system; Appendix B diagrams the electronic resource management workflow; Appendix D covers electronic resource management data elements; and Appendix E covers electronic resource management data structure. Appendix A from the report illustrates the detail and complexity involved in creating such a document. Figure 1.2 presented previously in Chapter 1 depicts another version of electronic resource management workflow. The DLF remains under the auspices of Council of Library and Information Resources and continues its work on the development of standards and best practices.

EDItEUR, an international organization, sponsors the development of standards for books, serials, and licensing terms and rights information with respect to the exchange of e-commerce data and rich metadata records. The electronic resource librarian would be interested in all ONIX standards, which are "designed to support computer-to-computer communication between parties involved in creating, distributing, licensing or otherwise making available intellectual property in published form, whether physical or digital" (EDItEUR 2015). The ERMS described earlier will ultimately incorporate these automated communications between a content provider's system and a library's systems, streamlining the administration of contract and license information.

Counting Online Usage of NeTworked Electronic Resources (COUN-TER) is a multiagency international initiative whose objective is to develop and maintain standards that "objective is to develop a set of internationally accepted, extendible Codes of Practice that allows the usage of online information products and services to be measured more consistently" (COUNTER 2015). The first COUNTER Code of Practice covered online journals and databases and was published in 2003. A revision in 2006 extended the standard to cover online books and reference works. COUNTER's work laid the foundation for the complementary standard SUSHI Protocol and the recommended practice COUNTER/SUSHI Implementation Profile. They work together to facilitate the automated harvesting and consolidation of usage statistics from different content providers in a consistent manner.

As is clear from this chapter, standards are the foundation of the products and processes used in information and technology-intensive fields. All participants in the information supply chain work together to develop best practices that facilitate the smooth operation of libraries. The electronic resource librarian will want to attend presentations and workshops by NISO at conferences such as Electronic Resources in Libraries (ERiL), the Charleston Conference, the NASIG annual conference, or the annual conference of the American Library Association. NISO gives presentations by active committees as well as a general "update" presentation. NISO encourages community engagement by sponsoring webinars and hosting a mailing list.

Additionally, the electronic resource librarian can work through their professional associations to engage in standards development work. These associations may be at the state level or consortial level or simply within the library's institution. Standards and best practices are developed at all organizational levels with the goal of improving the end-user experience. Since so much of that experience today is through digital systems and content, electronic resource librarians will find themselves on many committees.

ACTIVITIES

1. Choose a developed country other than the United States and determine the organization responsible for information standards. How is the organization structured? What is its relationship with other standards organizations at the

national and international levels? Research its information standards development process. How do they compare with NISO's?

2. Shared Electronic Resource Understanding (SERU) is a NISO Recommended
    Practice (RP-7–2012). Visit their workroom at http://www.niso.org/workrooms/
    seru/ and investigate how this best practice might be used in the place of formal
    licensing of electronic resources by libraries. Visit the SERU registry to deter-
    mine which publishers, content providers, and libraries participate. Consider
    why participation is not more universal.

REFERENCES

American National Standards Institute. 2015. "About ANSI." New York: American
    National Standards Institute. Retrieved from http://www.ansi.org/about_ansi/
    overview/overview.aspx?menuid=1.

Counting Online Usage of Networked Electronic Resources—COUNTER. 2015.
    "Homepage." Project COUNTER. Retrieved from http://www.projectcounter
    .org/index.html.

Digital Library Federation. 2004. "DLF Electronic Resource Management Initiative."
    Washington, DC: Council on Library and Information Resources. Retrieved
    from http://old.diglib.org/standards/dlf-erm02.htm.

EDItEUR. "ONIX." 2015. London: EDItEUR Limited. Retrieved from http://www
    .editeur.org/8/ONIX.

International Organization for Standardization. 2015a. "About ISO." Geneva:
    International Organization for Standardization. Retrieved from http://www.iso.
    org/iso/home/about.htm.

International Organization for Standardization. 2015b. "ISO/IEC JTC 1 Information
    technology." Geneva: International Organization for Standardization. Retrieved
    from http://www.iso.org/iso/home/standards_development/list_of_iso_technical_
    committees/iso_technical_committee.htm?commid=45020.

International Organization for Standardization. 2015c. "ISO/TC 46 Information
    and documentation." Geneva: International Organization for Standardization.
    Retrieved from http://www.iso.org/iso/home/standards_development/list_of_
    iso_technical_committees/iso_technical_committee.htm?commid=48750.

Jewell, T., et al. 2004. "Report of the DLF ERM Initiative." Washington, DC: Digi-
    tal Library Federation.

Koppel, T. 2008. "Standards, the Structural Underpinnings of Electronic Resource
    Management Systems." In *Electronic Resources in Libraries: Research and Prac-
    tice*, edited by Yu and Breivold. 295–306. Hershey, PA: Information Science
    Reference.

National Information Standards Organization. 2015a. "A Timeline of NISO Milestones." Baltimore: National Information Standards Organization. Retrieved from http://www.niso.org/about/NISO_milestone_timeline_fromISQ.pdf.

National Information Standards Organization. 2015b. "Welcome to NISO." Baltimore: National Information Standards Organization. Retrieved from http://www.niso.org/home.

National Information Standards Organization. 2015c. "Discovery to Delivery Topic Committee." Baltimore: National Information Standards Organization. Retrieved from http://www.niso.org/topics/d2d/.

National Information Standards Organization. 2015d. "Business Information Topic Committee." Baltimore: National Information Standards Organization. Retrieved from http://www.niso.org/topics/businfo/.

National Information Standards Organization. 2015e. "About TC46." Baltimore: National Information Standards Organization. Retrieved from http://www.niso.org/international/tc46/.

National Institute of Standards and Technology. 2013. "Public Law 104–113 National Technology Transfer and Advancement Act of 1995." Retrieved from http://www.nist.gov/standardsgov/nttaa-act.cfm.

Occupational Safety & Health Administration. 2015. "Regulations." Retrieved from https://www.osha.gov/pls/oshaweb/owadisp.show_document?p_table=STANDARDS&p_id=9698.

Pesch, O. 2008. "Library Standards and eResource Management: A Survey of Current Initiatives and Standards Efforts." *The Serials Librarian* 55 (3): 481–6.

FURTHER READING

NISO SERU Standing Committee. 2012. "NISO RP-7–2012, SERU: A Shared Electronic Resource Understanding." Baltimore: National Information Standards Organization. Retrieved from http://www.niso.org/workrooms/seru.

World Trade Organization. 2015. "Technical Barriers to Trade." Geneva: World Trade Organization. Retrieved from https://www.wto.org/english/tratop_e/tbt_e/tbt_e.htm.

Chapter 4
Identifying and Selecting Electronic Resources

Identifying and selecting electronic resources and the various systems used for resource delivery and management is a responsibility usually handled by a team of librarians that include subject specialists and systems personnel. Often, the electronic resource librarian will be the team leader in such a process since this is the person in the library with a holistic perspective on the resources and systems currently used by the library and those available in the marketplace. A keen analytical mind and the ability to organize thoughts and communicate them effectively are essential to this aspect of the position. The market for digital materials is large, and the variety of options for acquisition can be overwhelming. In addition to pinpointing the appropriate content, the electronic resource librarian will need to consider issues around licensing and cost. The electronic resource librarian must be able to evaluate the resource's usability and accessibility both within its own delivery system and as a potential component of the library's existing delivery systems.

Identifying and selecting new resources for a library's digital collection will almost always take place within the context of its existing resources. The process of assessing the effectiveness of current resources and systems to meet the needs of the community is a topic that will be addressed in Chapter 8. This chapter examines the formats of resources available in the marketplace, the acquisition models available, and approaches to evaluating the resources' suitability for a given library environment.

DEVELOPMENT OF DIGITAL FORMATS

Digital formats include databased indexes, full-text articles, electronic books, reference books, and streaming audio and visual databases. The first print library resources to be digitized were the discipline-based indexes. A subject index was once the primary entry point to academic journal literature. These extensive multivolume sets allowed users to find article citations in a subject area of interest. In the early days, these indexes were often compiled by professional organizations such as the Modern Language Association or the American Sociological Society to ensure that all of the important literature in their field was represented and was tagged with the appropriate subject terminology. Eventually, commercial firms began to specialize in index production and took over this work for many professional associations. Every library had its own set of indexes suited to its user community. These took up yards of shelf space, and they were cumbersome to use.

When technological opportunities to automate the storage and retrieval of bibliographic metadata surfaced, firms like DIALOG, described earlier, jumped in with both feet. DIALOG and the other early bibliographic databases were based on a pay-per-use model. While the librarian or end user would still need to take the citations retrieved, physically find the journals, and photocopy the articles, these databases presented a leap forward in the efficiency of scientific and medical research. It would be several years before the storage capacity of computing systems could accommodate the full text of journal articles.

A bibliographic database contains bibliographic records, much like an online catalog. In the context of electronic resource management, however, the records usually refer to journal and newspaper articles, conference proceedings, reports, government publications, and so on.

Bibliographic databases are still an important part of library collections, often fully integrated into content provider platforms, and providing a link to access the full text. The more common bibliographic databases will be included in content provider packages and will direct users to the full-text version of an article offered by that content provider before providing options to link out to different instances of a resource. More specialized bibliographic databases, such as Web of Science, offer not only indexing but also value rankings of articles, journals, and authors, among other things. These bibliographic databases are typically offered as a stand-alone product or are available only through one content provider.

As mentioned, as soon as computing capacity would allow, the full text of articles were being stored digitally. Initially, the articles were keyed into text files using American Standard Code for Information Interchange (ASCII). This, of course, led to typos and misspellings in the digital versions of the documents. They were still a welcome addition to the library collection.

Early attempts to digitize books involved keying the text into a digital file. Project Gutenberg is a notable example. Its founder, Michael Hart, was allotted $100,000,000 worth of computing time at the Materials Research Lab at the University of Illinois in 1971. To spend the allotment efficiently, he announced "that the greatest value created by computers would not be computing, but would be the storage, retrieval, and searching of what was stored in our libraries" (Hart 1992). He then proceeded to create electronic texts of public domain works, which now tally to more than 49,000.

Digital books were several years in the development/adoption phase. Readers were highly skeptical about the usability of digital text and were reluctant to adopt the early technologies. ASCII remained the predominant format for text until the 1990s as it was an open format that all operating systems could render. Software firms, such as Adobe, however, began working with software developers to ensure interoperability with its PDF or Portable Document Format, which presented text in a more professional and accessible manner. This was a welcome development for readers, but they still wanted the look and feel of a book. Attempts to make "paper" that would render text suitably failed, as did several early eReaders. Today, eReaders are commonplace, and few people have complaints about reading text on the screen of a personal device.

One of the first eReaders called the Rocket eBook was launched in 1998. It used proprietary software to render eBooks that could be purchased from Barnes and Noble. It was purported to be able to hold up to 10 eBooks. This wasn't too much of a problem, however, since there were very few digital books to download at the time.

The digital formats discussed thus far are bibliographic databases, full-text article databases, and electronic book databases. Reference works have also been digitized and often offer a multimedia experience with rich linking capabilities to related materials, vivid illustrations, and supplementary audio and video files. Multivolume bound reference works were once commonplace in the physical library. Like indexes, they took up considerable space. What's more, they quickly became outdated. Currency is one of the most important characteristics of reference works. Librarians would purchase updated versions of reference works annually or biennially. There was considerable cost associated with these acquisitions. The volumes were expensive not only to buy, but also to process time and time again.

Publishers that specialized in the production of reference works began to offer an online supplement to their print customers in the early 2000s. This development was appreciated by librarians as updated information would be available as it was written, rather than when the next edition arrived a year hence. Initially, these updates were primarily text based and not a suitable replacement for the image-rich reference works once lining the library shelves. As publishers pushed forward in developing their digital reference products, they were able to combine articles, images, images, statistics, and so on, from different but related print works to create customizable packages to accommodate different kinds of library audiences.

Currency and quality of the content were important, but so was usability. Reference librarians were experts in using the print reference works, and many preferred the print to their early digital counterparts. Statistical tables, for instance, were easier to use in the print. However, by the mid-2000s, the graphical user interfaces of digital reference works were much improved. Searches could be conducted across content sets and formats, enabling a much richer end-user experience. Audio and video files were introduced as complementary resources to the traditional text and image. A reference database might include audio files of rare interviews or videos demonstrating how to perform open-heart surgery.

Databases specializing in streaming audio and video have become commonplace in libraries, as well. Academic and school libraries at one time purchased educational videos for classroom use. Today, they can subscribe to a service that allows a professor to stream the videos from a content provider's site. Many public libraries now offer music services to their users, whereby a song can be streamed from the content provider's site. Some services will allow a limited number of periodic downloads of music to the library's end user. Libraries haven't worked out a deal with HBO or Netflix yet, but who knows what the future may hold. These resources and their means of delivery continue to evolve. It is an exciting time to be a librarian—and a library user, for that matter.

IDENTIFYING RESOURCES

Electronic resource librarians need to continually scan the environment to know about the products available to their libraries. Every vendor and publisher will have a blog, twitter feed, an email list for marketing purposes, or some combination of these, and librarians are welcome to engage. The larger content providers will offer product updates through webinars. Anyone can discover how to access these media outlets and educational opportunities by visiting the content provider's website. Word of mouth is also an important avenue for learning about products in development. Take the time to speak with content provider representatives at conferences, at consortia meetings, or in your library to find out what exciting products they have in the works. Networking with other electronic resource librarians is also an excellent way to keep apprised of new products and services.

An excellent resource to help the electronic resource librarian maintain currency in new digital products for libraries is the *Charleston Advisor*. It publishes critical reviews of online resources for libraries. The reviews are written by and peer-reviewed by professional librarians. In addition to a product description and critical evaluation, reviewers submit a composite score based on content, searchability, pricing, and contract options. Scoring is based on a five-star model with each component given equal weight. Guidelines for scoring follow.

- "Content
  - Special attention is paid to the intended audience for which the product is targeted—does the product meet the intended user needs? The content being compared with competitive products on the marketplace and any major omissions or special strengths will be factored into the rating.
- Searchability
  - The user interface and search engine are evaluated in terms of meeting the intended purposes. Is the product intuitive and easy-to-use? Are advanced searching features available if the product warrants it? Are graphics and other screen design features in keeping with the intent of the product and its audience? Is the search engine reliable and does it provide consistent results? Are there special features, installation requirements, plug-ins or other special software requirements? If so, is the product easy to use or more of a nuisance?
- Price
  - The value of the product in relation to its cost must be assessed. A high price alone does not necessarily mean a low ranking, but the product is evaluated in terms of content, user interface and value added features. However, content providers who resell duplicative content in different "packages," with enough difference to force libraries into acquiring these different packages, may be marked down. Content providers who are flexible (or inflexible) in their pricing options will be noted.
- Contract Options/Features
  - The contract provisions that accompany a service will be viewed in terms of accepted national guidelines (e.g. those adopted by major organizations such as the International Coalition of Library Consortia, Association of Research Libraries, ALA). Factors which might be considered include: definition of acceptable users, archiving provisions (when appropriate), lease / ownership of data, interlibrary loan provisions, redistribution of information provisions, or other peculiar or interesting issues." (Charleston Advisor 2015)

The Charleston Conference takes place annually in Charleston, South Carolina. It is an opportunity for publishers, vendors, and librarians to meet and discuss issues in content acquisition. Due to the conference's success, three associated publications are offered that continue these discussions throughout the year. *Against the Grain* is a publication for all interested parties. The *Charleston Advisor's* primary audience is librarians, and the *Charleston Report* is aimed at vendors and publishers.

Occasionally, the electronic resource librarian will be asked to identify options for accessing a specific journal or book not currently in the library's collection. *Books in Print* is a resource that "combines the most trusted and authoritative source of bibliographic information with powerful search, discovery and collection development tools designed specifically to streamline the book discovery and acquisition process. Libraries worldwide consult *Books In Print* to find titles, create lists and decide from *Books In Print's* vast inventory of files which vendor, eBook platform or online retailer to source the title" (Books in Print 2015). Ulrich's Web is a similar resource for discovering in which databases a given journal title might be found. Both products are affiliated with ProQuest, LLC.

SELECTING ELECTRONIC RESOURCES

It may be tempting to identify a product that meets the subject needs of your library, determine that it is well regarded through reviews, discover that it fits the library's budgetary parameters, and give it a green light. However, the electronic resource librarian must take into account many more considerations before making a recommendation. The first thing to consider is whether the product is unique or is one of several comparable products. If this is the case, determine the reliability and authority of the respective producers. Compare the depth of coverage, as well as the currency, accuracy, and quality of information. Discover whether the content represents the appropriate intellectual level for your library's customers. Usually there is enough differentiation between comparable products to be able to pinpoint the one best suited to a given library.

The desired product may be offered through more than one channel. For instance, a package of journal titles from a publisher may be made available by nonexclusive licenses through several database platforms. It is not uncommon to see journal holdings replicated among the largest content providers. To determine which platform is best suited for the library's purposes, start by considering the content provider's primary audience. The same content may be available through different interfaces and in combination with different complementary resources. For instance, a database of medical information may be offered through an interface intended for nurses, which allows linking to pharmaceutical information and patient care videos. The same database of medical information might be made available through a patient-oriented site with options for community networking.

If it has been determined that the content is appropriate, the electronic resource librarian can continue the evaluation of the resource or comparable resources by considering certain technical, business, and usability aspects. These considerations parallel those used by the *Charleston Advisor* in their reviews. The emphasis here, however, is the resource's suitability to the specific library's ecosystem, rather than the general library audience.

Every database sits behind a delivery platform. These platforms are often associated with the content provider's brand, such as EBSCOHost. Occasionally, a database will be offered through a less robust search and retrieval tool produced by the publisher of the content. The larger content providers, EBSCOHost, ProQuest LLC, Elsevier, and so on, tend to have more robust technological features and have adopted industry standards for efficient performance and interoperability with other systems. However, smaller providers, such as Alexander Street Press, Johns Hopkins University Press, or Oxford University Press, should not be dismissed as they tend to have high quality and unique content, and they offer exceptional customer service. From a technical standpoint, the electronic resource librarian will want to ensure that a delivery platform meets the following minimum requirements:

- It permits local customization and branding through administration permissions; it authenticates users by IP address (rather than passwords) and is compatible with proxy services.
- It is compatible with the library's existing and/or future software systems, including the knowledge base, link resolver, discovery layer, and electronic resource management system.
- It provides COUNTER-compliant usage statistics through a SUSHI schema.

The electronic resource librarian has to consider many licensing options typically available by a content provider within the context of their library. Licensing will be covered in greater detail in the following chapter, but for purposes of evaluation, common contractual arrangements will be introduced here. Journal database vendors will most often offer a one or multiyear subscription to a set of content. Sometimes, content can be licensed for perpetual access as long as the library agrees to pay an annual fee for the use of the content provider's search interface. Occasionally, content can be "purchased" and be made available through a search interface maintained by the library. Individual journals may also be offered to the library directly from a publisher or through a vending service such as EBSCO Online.

eBooks have been adopted by library users, and librarians are trying to accommodate demand. eBooks are available from aggregators and directly from publishers. Not every book is available from both types of sources however. And every eBook is usually not available from every aggregator. This results in a situation where a library must use multiple suppliers in order to achieve a comprehensive coverage of eBooks. It is a challenge to determine which titles will be available on which platform. A benefit resulting from the surge in eBook publishing is that a new model of acquisition, Demand-Driven Acquisition (DDA), has developed to aid librarians in selecting items that their users want to use.

This more recent trend in the "acquisition" of eBooks, the move to DDA, offers librarians several options if they choose to work with a DDA model. They can contract directly with suppliers or they can work with publishers and aggregators through an approval plan. Three common platform types are available: commercial aggregator platforms, not-for-profit or university press platforms, and publisher platforms. Some aggregators have been offering DDA for a decade or more through their journal databases and often can provide a seamless unmediated process for the end user and a streamlined, efficient administrative portal for the librarian. As the technologies for providing resources on demand matures, the other content providers will adopt them.

All of these licensing possibilities may seem overwhelming. However, choices are often made easier to navigate. Positive relationships that already exist between a content provider and a library often result in extending that relationship with an additional resource. The collection development librarians may already use a given service for selection and would be most comfortable using an approval plan through that familiar interface. Libraries often engage in collaborative "acquisition" of digital content. The options offered to member libraries by a consortium are usually already pared down to those most suited to its members.

TRIALING THE RESOURCE

If the resource or resources under consideration pass muster with the library's content needs and technical requirements, and offers contracting options suitable to the library's business practices, the next step in evaluation would be to test the product. Setting up a trial consumes valuable time and energy from the library and the content provider. As such, it is important to have thoroughly vetted the resources against the previously outlined criteria before proceeding to trial. Implementing a trial may be straightforward if the library already offers databases through the platform used by the resource under consideration. In other cases, library personnel may need to go through many of the steps of access provision just as if the resources had already been "acquired"; see Chapter 6 for more information. On the bright side, if the library decides to acquire, then the initial setup will be less time consuming.

Once a trial is set up with the content provider, and the resource implemented in house, the electronic resource librarian should test the product to ensure that it is operating seamlessly with the other library systems before announcing the trial. Libraries will have different policies regarding the process of trialing. Some library policies will be to make an announcement to the community at large and provide a means for users to give feedback. Other library policies have a more targeted approach and will direct a gathering of feedback from a committee dedicated to developing electronic collections and possibly from a focused group of end users. In smaller libraries, the electronic resource librarian may be left to complete the evaluation unilaterally. In any of these cases, evaluation will proceed in a similar way.

During the trial, the electronic resource librarian has the opportunity to ensure that the content provided by the resource is in fact as described in the content provider's marketing materials. It is also an opportunity to test the usability of the content provider platform with this product. Even if the librarian is already familiar with the interface, it is important to test the compatibility of the database and its metadata with the search and retrieval system. Content providers that aggregate disparate databases are often met with the challenge of mapping metadata to common indexes. While content providers attempt to achieve this mapping as cleanly as possible, it can result in confusing and inconsistent search options and results. At a minimum, the following usability considerations should be checked.

- It should have noticeable and useful on-screen help and/or tutorials.
- It should have an approachable basic search interface for a novice user.
- Advanced searching options are available for researchers and professional librarians if the content warrants.
- Descriptive metadata is accurate, complete, and consistent.
- The resource, in whatever format, loads in a timely manner and is easily rendered.
- Error messages are noticeable and helpful, indicating specific problems and solutions.
- There should be the ability to save, print, and email metadata records, as well as the actual resource, if applicable.

Once a resource has been trialed, electronic resource librarians will gather feedback from various vested parties to augment their own evaluation. They would then write a recommendation to the selection committee. Unless the committee has trialed two databases with similar content for the purposes of comparison, the committee's deliberations should be straightforward at this point. If the trial was not a success, the committee may decide to continue the trial for an additional period of time or to discontinue the acquisitions process. If the trial was a success, the electronic resource librarian will notify the content provider representative and proceed to the process of reviewing the license and considering various contract options. Chapter 5 introduces the reader to concepts and best practices that the electronic resource librarian will find essential for a successful license review and negotiation.

ACTIVITY

1. Identify and evaluate a product available through your library that offers resources in a format of interest. Write a review in the style of the *Charleston Advisor*. Some items, like price and contract options, may not be available to you. Sometimes, general terms and pricing are available. Limit your review to 1,000 words. Be sure to include a comprehensive score. Exchange reviews with a partner and provide written critiques and suggestions to improve the review.

REFERENCES

The Charleston Advisor. 2015. "TCA Scoring Guide." Denver: The Charleston Advisor. Retrieved from http://charlestonco.com/index.php?do=About+TCA&pg=ScoringGuide.

Hart, M. 1992. "The History and Philosophy of Project Gutenberg." Salt Lake City: Project Gutenberg. Retrieved from http://www.gutenberg.org/wiki/Gutenberg:About.

FURTHER READING

Center for Research Libraries. 2015. "Academic Database Assessment Tool." Retrieved from http://adat.crl.edu/databases#results.

Chapter 5
Acquiring and Licensing Electronic Resources

Once an electronic resource librarian determines that a resource is appropriate to add to the library's electronic collections, work begins with the acquisitions department to ensure that all of the institution's requirements are met during the licensing and contract negotiation process.

It is understandable that the profession continues to call the process of obtaining a license "an acquisition." Many of the transactional workflows are the same as they were with acquired physical copies of intellectual content including ordering, invoicing, and cataloging. However, this is where the similarities end; the areas of selection, evaluation/assessment, discovery, access, delivery, and preservation are radically different between owned physical copies and licensed digital copies. Even if a library were to obtain a license for perpetual access of a digital copy of a resource, the laws around how a library can treat that resource are different. The first-sale doctrine does not apply to licensed copies as it does to an owned copy of a physical document. Libraries acquire and purchase licenses, not resources.

Acquiring copies of copyrighted works through purchase affords the owner of the copy certain rights under the first-sale doctrine found in Section 109 of Title 17 of the U.S. Code. These rights, which include the ability of the copy owner to rent or lease that copy, are what has afforded libraries in America the ability to lend the copies of the materials they own to the communities they serve without obtaining additional permissions from the copyright holder of the work. For the first-sale doctrine to apply to a copy of a work, it needs to be on a medium that cannot be easily copied. While many electronic materials will have embedded digital rights management protections that prevent unauthorized copying, copyright owners will ensure further protection by explicitly licensing the work rather than selling a copy of it. Section 109 d affords this protection:

> The privileges prescribed by subsections (a) and (c) do not, unless authorized by the copyright owner, extend to any person who has acquired possession of the copy or phonorecord from the copyright owner, by rental, lease, loan, or otherwise, without acquiring ownership of it.

Further complicating the ability of a library to acquire a copy of an electronic resource is the distance of the library from the copyright holder in the information supply chain. The licensing of copyrights requires that the licensor has copyrights to license. The original copyrights holder is the creator of the work. The creator may transfer their copyrights in any number of combinations to a party, such as a publisher. The publisher, in turn, when contracting with a vendor may transfer only those rights that it has negotiated with the creator. Often these agreements are time sensitive and involve collections of works generally rather than specific copyrighted titles. For a vendor, then, to be able to transfer a copy for the purposes of ownership to a library is unlikely. A scenario in which a library could purchase digital copies of a work would need to be negotiated with a party closer to the source, such as the creator.

CONTRACT BASICS

A license is a type of contract, which is a binding legal agreement that is enforceable in a court of law. To be valid and enforceable, it must be a consensual exchange between competent parties. The transaction must be an offer and acceptance of an offer as well as an exchange of consideration, that is, something of value. The parties to the contract must have legal capacity; that is, they are of legal age and of sound mind, and they must be negotiating in good faith with the purpose of becoming legally bound. There can be no misrepresentation or coercion. All of these pieces must be in place, or the contract may be voidable.

If a party to a contract inadvertently or intentionally did not comply with the requirements mentioned earlier, the offended party may declare the contract void. Examples of reasons that a contract may be voided are:

- Oversight or misunderstanding
- Incompetence or incapacity
- Duress or undue influence
- Unconscionably unfair terms
- Fraud and misrepresentation

If one or the other party to a contract does not make good on their promise or prevents other parties from making good on a promise, then they are considered to be in breach of the contract. Remedies include specific performance, which means forcing the breaching party to make good on the promise or damages may be awarded. These are usually monetary.

Contract law is state law with state jurisdiction, interpretation, and application. Every contract will have a clause specifying the state under which it will be interpreted and adjudicated if necessary. In many cases, contract law is uniform to facilitate interstate business. An example of this kind of attempt at harmonization is the Uniform Commercial Code. In addition to the specification of state jurisdiction, all contracts tend to have a set of common clauses that you will see again and again, sometimes called boilerplate clauses. These clauses have little to do with the specific exchange of consideration between the parties. Instead, they deal with how the contract will be enforced and how disputes will be resolved. Boilerplate clauses often found in a license for an electronic resource include the following:

- Arbitration. This clause refers to whether a dispute about the contract will be resolved through arbitration proceedings, rather than through a lawsuit.
- Choice of law. This clause determines which state's legal rules will be applied in a lawsuit in the event of a dispute.
- Confidentiality. This clause ensures that the parties to the contract will not disclose certain information.
- Force majeure. This clause establishes that the agreement will be suspended in the event of unforeseen disasters or "acts of God," such as an earthquake or flood.
- Indemnity. This clause establishes which party to the contract will cover the costs of disputes brought by third parties.
- Jurisdiction. This clause determines in which state and county a lawsuit must be filed in the event of a dispute.

- Limitations on damages. This clause limits the amount and types of damages that may be awarded in a contract dispute.
- Notice. This clause describes how each party must provide notice to the other, in the event that there will be a change to the agreement.
- Severability. This clause permits a court to remove an invalid provision in the contract, leaving the remaining parts of the contract intact.
- Signature authority. This clause warrants that the individuals who sign the contract do, in fact, have the authority to represent and bind their respective parties to the agreement.
- Waiver. This clause permits the parties to give up the right to sue for breach of a particular provision of the agreement without giving up any future claims regarding the same provision.
- Warranties. This clause provides assurances by each party regarding its various contract obligations.

LICENSING BEST PRACTICES

Fortunately, electronic resource librarians have many resources available to aid in the process of license review and negotiation. Unlike the purchasing of physical resources, which is held to uniform terms, provisions for licensing electronic resources are variable and should be scrutinized before an agreement is finalized. The clauses of a typical license have become fairly standardized over the past two decades. Guidance from professional organizations such as the Association of Research Libraries (ARL) and the Center for Research Libraries has provided recommendations for sound practice. The National Information Standards Organization (NISO) has also published a recommended practice, RP-7–2012, called the Shared Electronic Resource Understanding (SERU).

As explained by ARL in its 1997 document titled Principles for Licensing Electronic Resources, the electronic resource librarian will seldom be expected to sign a license with a vendor on behalf of the institution

> Given the obligations that a contract creates for an institution and the possible liability associated with not meeting those obligations, most institutions will delegate the authority to sign contracts to a specific office or officer within the institution. In many institutions, this signatory authority will reside in the purchasing department, legal counsel's or vice president's office, or the library director's office, although in some institutions, a library staff member may be granted authority for signing license agreements. Nevertheless, library staff will often be responsible for initial review

and negotiation of the material terms of the license because they have the most knowledge of the user community and of the resource being acquired. Library staff should be well informed of the uses critical to the library's user community (e.g., printing, downloading, and copying). (ARL 1997)

The 15 principles they set forth in the very early days of library/vendor contracts follow:

1. A license agreement should state clearly what access rights are being acquired by the licensee—permanent use of the content or access rights only for a defined period of time.
2. A license agreement should recognize and not restrict or abrogate the rights of the licensee or its user community permitted under copyright law. The licensee should make clear to the licensor those uses critical to its particular users including, but not limited to, printing, downloading, and copying.
3. A license agreement should recognize the intellectual property rights of both the licensee and the licensor.
4. A license agreement should not hold the licensee liable for unauthorized uses of the licensed resource by its users, as long as the licensee has implemented reasonable and appropriate methods to notify its user community of use restrictions.
5. The licensee should be willing to undertake reasonable and appropriate methods to enforce the terms of access to a licensed resource.
6. A license agreement should fairly recognize those access enforcement obligations which the licensee is able to implement without unreasonable burden. Enforcement must not violate the privacy and confidentiality of authorized users.
7. The licensee should be responsible for establishing policies that create an environment in which authorized users make appropriate use of licensed resources and for carrying out due process when it appears that a use may violate the agreement.
8. A license agreement should require the licensor to give the licensee notice of any suspected or alleged license violations that come to the attention of the licensor and allow a reasonable time for the licensee to investigate and take corrective action, if appropriate.
9. A license agreement should not require the use of an authentication system that is a barrier to access by authorized users.
10. When permanent use of a resource has been licensed, a license agreement should allow the licensee to copy data for the purposes of preservation and/or the creation of a usable archival copy. If a license agreement does not permit the licensee to make a usable preservation copy, a license agreement should specify who has permanent archival responsibility for the resource and under what conditions the licensee may access or refer users to the archival copy.

11. The terms of a license should be considered fixed at the time the license is signed by both parties. If the terms are subject to change (for example, scope of coverage or method of access), the agreement should require the licensor or licensee to notify the other party in a timely and reasonable fashion of any such changes before they are implemented and permit either party to terminate the agreement if the changes are not acceptable.

12. A license agreement should require the licensor to defend, indemnify, and hold the licensee harmless from any action based on a claim that use of the resource in accordance with the license infringes any patent, copyright, trademark, or trade secret of any third party.

13. The routine collection of use data by either party to a license agreement should be predicated upon disclosure of such collection activities to the other party and must respect laws and institutional policies regarding confidentiality and privacy.

14. A license agreement should not require the licensee to adhere to unspecified terms in a separate agreement between the licensor and a third party unless the terms are fully reiterated in the current license or fully disclosed and agreed to by the licensee.

15. A license agreement should provide termination rights that are appropriate to each party. (ARL 1997)

These are excellent general guidelines for the electronic resource librarian to consider when reviewing a license for the first time. These emphasize areas that could potentially affect the end-user experience. These are areas of the license that an institution's attorney might not look at closely. However, from the library's perspective, these 15 points represent some of the more important language in the contract. There will be much more information to read through before approving the license for the library. Lipinsky (2013) has written an exhaustive work on licensing for librarians. Liblicense also is an outstanding reference resource that is continually updated and provides a wealth of useful information. Its Licensing Vocabulary page provides an alphabetical list of terms often used in library/vendor licenses, along with their definition.

DIGITAL CONTENT LICENSE PROVISIONS

The licenses that the electronic resource librarian will review will have a number of similarities. In addition to the standard clauses found in contracts, generally, licenses to access digital content will all share a number of standard clauses as well. While all of these provisions should be checked for accuracy, special attention should be given to the areas of authorized use and the performance obligations of the parties to the license.

Standard Clauses

The following list comprises a number of clauses that the electronic resource librarian will encounter in a license review:

- Parties to the agreement.
  - Licensor is the vendor and licensee is the library or parent institution.
  - Legal entities authorized to enter into a contract.
  - Legal names and addresses.
- Definitions.
  - All terms that are interpreted in any way other than a dictionary meaning.
  - Common defined terms are authorized uses, authorized users, commercial use, content, interlibrary loan, licensed content, premises, territory.
- Subject matter or product definition.
  - Be as explicit as possible.
  - May be put in an appendix.
- Fair use/fair dealing provision.
  - If the license does not explicitly address fair use, then copyright law principles apply.
  - Even if it explicitly restricts fair use, the restriction applies to licensee, not the end user.
- License fee.
  - Subscription model—unlimited or limited use, payment schedule, access fees.
- Duration of license.
  - Usually a specific length of time, often aligning with the fiscal routines of the licensee.
  - Automatic renewal if all are satisfied.
  - Request notice of changes in price or license terms.
  - Automatic increase in price tied to an "inflation" rate.
  - Requires diligent monitoring.
- Termination rights.
  - Breach of contract—ensures prorated refund in the event of early termination.
- Archiving and perpetual access.
  - Library makes one—consider the costs.

Authorized Users

This provision describes who may access licensed information and from where or through what means they can access it. The authorized users will depend on the type of library and its organizational affiliations. While it is important to be as inclusive as possible when defining potential users, the electronic resource librarian needs to be mindful that license fees are based in part on the number and distribution of the user base. An academic librarian will want to ensure that students, faculty, staff, alumni, and affiliated users are expressly identified. Also, public colleges and universities will want to ensure that members of the public who use the library on-site may have access. A corporate library may only need two or three simultaneous access seats. A public library will certainly want to ensure that all visitors to the physical library can use the resource and that remote use is available to all registered borrowers. A school library media center will need to negotiate access for all students and staff on-site and also for remote access for teachers, and possibly the parents of the students. Consortium-wide licenses will need to consider a wide sweep of potential users.

Most electronic resources are hosted by the vendor at a remote location and will be accessed by users through the Internet. To ensure that the user trying to access the resource is authorized, there must be a system in place for identifying and authenticating him or her. Most database vendors will have the technological capacity to identify Internet Protocol (IP) addresses and will prefer to use this method. Librarians also prefer this method as it provides more seamless access to the end user. The institution will have a range of association IP addresses, and its proxy server for authenticating off-site users will be within that range. This is the most widely used model, but there are other, less common means of authentication, which will be discussed in Chapter 6. Smaller resource providers might require that authorized users enter a username and password to access the content.

Authorized Use

The provisions describing the authorized use of licensed information are central to the license agreement. These identify how the information can be used once it is accessed. A number of issues need to be kept in mind when negotiating use. First, identify which uses are expressly permitted and which are expressly restricted. Typically, those permitted include any use that is not intended for commercial gain, such as noncommercial, educational, personal, and research. Within these parameters, users of the resource will have the right to retrieve, transmit, reproduce, store, and print the material. There will likely be restrictions or limitations on these uses however, such as prohibiting systematic copying or transmission, the modification of content, or the creation of derivatives. Vendors will often also declare restrictions on the transferability and sublicensing of the material for good measure.

The license may be silent on some uses that are of interest to the library. The omission of specifics on use in a license is interpreted by many to be an indication that in those unspecified situations, copyright law would apply. That is, unless otherwise stated, all of the limitations to a copyright holder's exclusive rights, such as fair use, or the reproduction by libraries and archives, prevail. Still, institutions with legal arms, such as universities and municipalities, are more comfortable with explicit statements of use in certain areas including interlibrary loan (ILL), course packs, and distribution or performance of resources in a distance learning environment. Some electronic resource librarians prefer to have language for these uses as well as any uses that may yet be unidentified. A final important component of this area of the license is determining how unauthorized use will be handled, if it were to occur.

Licensee and Licensor Obligations

Beyond paying the invoice, much of the library's obligations involve making reasonable assurances that the users and use of the resource are authorized. The library cannot be expected to guarantee anything. Some of the reasonable steps that the library is expected to take are to keep the roster of authorized users up to date. The library will be expected to notify users of the rights regarding the use of the licensed content. This usually can be accomplished by posting verbiage at access points to the resource and by posting information at physical terminals in the library and other areas within the institution. The library, often through the institution's IT office, will also need to monitor the data coming and going through the servers for unusual activity, that is, unexpectedly heavy data flow indicating possible systematic downloading. If this type of activity does occur, it is likely that the vendor will become aware of it before the library and will take immediate action to stop the breach. Finally, the library or the IT department will be expected to maintain Internet use statistics. These statistics should be anonymized so that user privacy is protected.

Licensors tend to have more obligations detailed in the contract. This is, after all, the details about the products and services that are being licensed. The product description will have already been laid out, but it will be reiterated here along with information about the hosting capacity of the vendor. As is often the case, the licensed resource is maintained externally by the vendor; they should assure libraries that the resource will be delivered, to the degree possible, in a complete and uninterrupted fashion. Not every situation can be predicted or prevented, so an outright guarantee of uninterrupted service is unlikely. Although licensors are unlikely to guarantee uninterrupted service, librarians should expect vendors to take appropriate measures to mitigate service interruptions. Emery and Stone (2013) suggest that vendors assure that they will:

- Have adequate backup servers in the event the main server crashes
- Have appropriate hardware to handle a minimum number of simultaneous users
- Designate downtime exceeding certain specified amounts as unreasonable or unacceptable
- Provide specifications for the adjustment or rebate of the subscription cost in the event of unreasonable interruptions in service. (Emery and Stone 2013)

The vendor will also make certain assurances regarding the quality, quantity, and currency of the content provided through the licensed resource. First of all, the licensor should ensure that they do, in fact, have the rights to license the content, and in a case where this is not so, they should explicitly indemnify the library of any breaches. Librarians do not expect that the content in the database will remain static, but they do want to know that the library's investment will not be substantially diminished over the course of the license. If a substantive change is expected, such as the removal of significant titles or the reduction of holdings for a given title, it is important that licensees be notified in a timely manner. How this notification will occur should be explicit in the license agreement. Where such changes significantly affect the quality of the licensed information, the agreement should provide for an adjustment to the subscription fees.

FINALIZING THE AGREEMENT

The electronic resource librarian may have an ongoing cordial relationship with the vendor already. Smaller vendors may not even wish to bother with a license. As mentioned in Chapter 3, a recommended practice exists that eliminates the need for a license if both parties are amenable. This alternative is called the Shared Electronic Resource Understanding (SERU)—National Information Standards Organization (NISO) RP-7–2012. It is a standard license that articulates business practices and relies on copyright law to govern the use of the digital content being licensed. Organizations that have an interest in using SERU sign onto a registry. Signing the registry, however, does not obligate a library or content provider to use the SERU license in every circumstance.

One of the more elusive areas of license negotiation is determining how much your institution should pay for access to the resource. Librarians do not typically discuss the pricing around their electronic resources outside of their own institution or consortium. There are many factors that determine pricing, such as the number of users, the length of the contract, and whether the resource is part of a larger package. These differences make it difficult to compare pricing from one institution to another. The electronic resource librarian can find some guidance, however. Resources such as Allen Press's ongoing study of subscription prices or the periodical price survey published by the *Library Journal* provide information on journal pricing trends.

As is evident, there is much to consider when reviewing a license. Fortunately, there are plenty of professional resources at the electronic resource librarian's disposal to assist him or her with the review. Once the license has been thoroughly reviewed and pricing terms negotiated, it can then be sent to the appropriate parties for their signatures. The next step in the process is to make the resource accessible to the end user. This set of activities will be covered in Chapter 6.

ACTIVITIES

1. Select an electronic resource that makes its generic license available through the Internet. Compare it with the model license maintained at the Liblicense website at http://liblicense.crl.edu/licensing-information/publishers-licenses/.
   a. Are there significant differences in the provisions or language used?
   b. Evaluate the impact these differences might have on the operations of a library type of your choice.
2. Review the two most recent updates of Allen Press's Study of Subscription Prices for Scholarly Society Journals. The 2015 version can be downloaded at http://allenpress.com/resources/education/jps.

a. What are the common themes addressed in both reports? How have perceptions changed around these themes over time? What are possible causes for the change in perception?

b. What themes are present in one and not the other report? Why was that topic of interest only in a particular time period?

REFERENCES

Association of Research Libraries, et al. 1997. "Principles for Licensing Electronic Resources." Washington, DC: Association of Research Libraries. Retrieved from http://www.arl.org/storage/documents/publications/licensing-principles-1997.pdf.

Center for Research Libraries. "LibLicense: Licensing Digital Content—A Resource for Libraries." Chicago: Center for Research Libraries. Retrieved from http://liblicense.crl.edu/.

Emery, L., and G. Stone. "Acquisition of New Content." In *Techniques for Electronic Resource Management*. *Library Technology Reports*, February/March 2013. Chicago: American Library Association.

FURTHER READING

Center for Research Libraries. "LibLicense: Publisher's Licenses." Chicago: Center for Research Libraries, 2015. Retrieved from http://liblicense.crl.edu/licensing-information/publishers-licenses/.

Lipinsky, T. A. *The Librarian's Legal Companion for Licensing Information Resources and Services*. Chicago: Neal Schuman, an imprint of the American Library Association, 2013.

National Information Standards Organization. "SERU Recommended Practice (RP-7–2012)." Baltimore: National Information Standards Organization, 2015. Retrieved from http://www.niso.org/workrooms/seru.

Chapter 6
Providing Access to Electronic Resources

This chapter explains the provision of access to electronic resource and discusses how access to electronic resources differs from access to physical resources. Providing access to physical library resources is straightforward; "mark it and park it" is a phrase that is sometimes used to describe an approach to organizing physical resources in a library. It refers to attaching a classification or call number to an item and to the bibliographic record that represents that item in the library catalog, mark it, and then placing the item on the shelf, park it, for customers to find, check out, use, and so on. From this perspective, "Nothing else is needed to move a book from acquisitions through binding and labeling to storage, into the hands of the patron and back again" (Bade 2007, 4). Little or no additional infrastructure is required to use the contents of the physical information resource. Whether it is being used to convey information or as a doorstop, a printed book is usable with no other equipment. A CD or DVD requires a player in order to hear and/or view its content, but these players have been standardized and are readily available in most personal computing systems. This is not necessarily the case with other types of electronic resources.

Electronic resources require external equipment, as well as hardware and software to identify, find, select, obtain and render their contents. Consider the example of a college student who needs to find and read journal articles for a term paper. The first task is to find articles on the topic of the paper. The Student might turn to a library database or to Google or Google Scholar, but it is very unlikely that they would turn to a printed index in order to find journal content. Whether using a library database or Google, the student will need a computer. In the broad sense, this includes everything from a desktop computer to a smartphone, Internet service, and software to perform the search. Assuming that a student has these things, he or she conducts a search and finds among the search results citations to or even links to the full text of several useful articles. In order to read the articles, the student will need yet more software. Moreover, the type of software needed is dictated by the format in which the article is encoded; if it is in pdf format, it will require the Adobe Reader software; if it is in word processing format, word processing software is needed to read it; if it is in ePub format, one of several types of ePub reader/viewers is needed, and so on.

We are assuming the student in our example has access to the full text of the articles in the search results. This depends on the licensing agreements made with the content providers as covered in Chapter 5. It is usually safe to suppose that the results of a search of a library catalog can be obtained from the library, that is, that the library owns and has permission to lend the items represented in the search results.

In the United States, permission to lend library materials is usually assumed based on what is called the first-sale doctrine as it is described in the U.S. copyright law (17 U.S.C. § 109(a)).

This is not the case with electronic resources. The database being searched may be "proprietary." This means that the database is produced by an external entity like a publisher or aggregator, giving it certain intellectual property rights some of which are licensed to the library, usually for a subscription fee. The database may also be freely available or open source, providing freely available or open access content. Regardless of whether the platform is proprietary or open, the records retrieved may or may not link to the full text of a resource. For example, if a student is using the freely available Google Scholar search and retrieval tool, the results of a search might not yield records pointing to freely available full text.

The use of proprietary platforms and the resources therein provided by content providers is usually governed by a license agreement. This license may be more restrictive than copyright law regarding the uses to which the platform and full text materials it contains may be put. One very common license restriction specifies who can use the electronic resource. This restriction usually describes the library's customers in a way that excludes people who are not affiliated with the institution. In the case of an academic library, it includes the students enrolled there and the faculty who teach there. In the case of the public library, it excludes those who do not hold a valid library card. School libraries, as other academic institutions, include the teachers and students attending the school. It also almost always puts the onus on librarians to enforce this restriction. What this means in terms of providing access to library-subscribed electronic resources is that the library must find a way to provide access only to authorized users, which is often done using authentication and proxy servers.

This chapter examines ways in which the unique characteristics of electronic resources impact the provision of access to electronic resources by libraries. This is the "Provide Access" and "Administer" steps in the electronic resources life cycle illustrated in Figure 1.2. It covers registering IP addresses with content providers, registration of individual electronic journals, and the management of authentication and proxy services; knowledge bases, A-to-Z lists, and link resolvers will be covered in Chapter 7.

ADMINISTRATIVE MODULE MANAGEMENT

An administrative module is a web-based tool provided by almost all electronic resource vendors and publishers that allows a member of a subscribing library's staff to manage or administer the library's electronic resource subscription(s). Managing an electronic resource subscription includes activities like

- Customizing the search experience to the needs of the library's customers
- Viewing lists of titles included in a particular electronic resource
- Generating reports that describe how the library's customers are using the resource, registering the library's ownership of specific electronic content
- Communicating to the resource vendor information required for authenticating authorized library customers

- Communicating to the resource vendor information about the library's local collection for the display of local holdings in search results
- Branding the appearance of the resource with the library's logo

The specific activities will vary depending on the type of content included in the electronic resource. For example, the activities related to managing a resource that contains eBooks will be slightly different from those related to managing an electronic journal subscription. Both of these will be slightly different from the activities related to managing a resource that contains a journal index and full text articles.

Each content provider has its own administrative module. It is not uncommon for a library to subscribe to more than one electronic resource from a single content provider. In that case, library staff uses a single administrative module to manage all of the electronic resources on that platform. For example, an academic library might subscribe to Academic Search Complete, Library Literature & Information Science Full Text, SocINDEX with Full Text, and Agricola from Ebsco Information Services. The library staff member charged with managing these resources would use a single administrative module on Ebsco's website to manage all four resources. A public library would be more likely to subscribe to Library Literature & Information Science Full Text, while a school library would need Education Index for its teachers.

Most libraries subscribe to electronic resources through more than one content provider, which means that library staff must work with multiple administrative modules all of which may be slightly different. The activities are generally the same such as customizing the customer experience, branding, and generating reports, but different content providers may use different terminologies and different functionalities to accomplish them. Thus, it is very useful to understand the process of managing a library's electronic resources using content provider administrative modules.

ENTRY URLS AND ACCESS TO THE ADMINISTRATIVE MODULE

Once the license agreement has been signed and payment made, it is time to implement a newly purchased/subscribed electronic resource. The library should receive a URL from the content provider that points to the default entry page to the resource, a URL from the content provider that points to their administrative module, and a username and password for access to the administrative module. The URL that points to the default entry page is the one the library will use on its web pages, Database A-to-Z lists, catalog, and so on, to direct customers to the resource. The URL that points to the administrative module with the username and password should not be shared with customers but should be shared with all library staff who are responsible for managing aspects of electronic resources life cycle.

One person, often a head of the department in the library who is responsible for electronic resources, has top administrator privileges for managing a content provider's administrative module. Some administrative modules may allow the top administrator to create lower-level administrative roles for additional library staff members depending on their responsibilities. For example, a reference librarian might need access to the administrative module in order to help a customer troubleshoot a problem with a particular electronic resource. They might need to be able to see a list of titles included in the resource or check to see whether the content provider is experiencing downtime. That person might be given read-only access to the administrative module. Someone responsible for maintaining the library's IP addresses, explained more fully later, might need read and write permissions to the section of the administrative module where the library's IP addresses are maintained but might not need any access to the section where usage reports are generated.

It is important to note that most librarians find it prudent to limit the number of those with access to administrative modules to a few. The more library staff with access to administrative modules, the greater the chances for miscommunication and changes to electronic resources that may create barriers to customer access. A clear strong electronic resource management policy is very useful for preventing these accidents. Many libraries are also using an internal database called an electronic resource management system (ERMS) as a tool for communicating among staff responsible for electronic resource management as well as a tool for recording information about electronic resources subscriptions such as URLS, usernames, and passwords.

REGISTRATION AND LOCAL COLLECTIONS

Libraries subscribe to collections of electronic journals including aggregations and publisher-specific collections as a means of providing customer access to a large number of journals at an affordable price. The affordable price, usually much lower than subscribing to each journal in the collection individually, is the main advantage of this purchasing model. The disadvantage is that if and when librarians decide to cancel a subscription to the collection, they and their customers will lose access to all of the subscribed content meaning back issues of content as well as the current year.

Most libraries subscribe to some journals individually through a subscription agent, mostly in electronic format, because those journals are important to the library's customers. The disadvantage is that if and when librarians decide to cancel its subscription to the collection, depending on the license terms, they and their customers may lose access to all of the subscribed content, meaning back issues of content as well as the current year.

Access to individual electronic journal subscriptions may be through a portal provided by the subscription agent or through the publisher's website or both. The subscription agent usually manages access to electronic journal content through a web portal; this constitutes part of the added value subscription agents provide to libraries. But when access to the electronic journal is through the publisher's website, the library may need to communicate to or verify its subscription with the publisher in order to obtain access to it. Registration of an individual electronic journal refers to the process of communicating to a publisher the subscription information received from the subscription agent.

Because individual subscriptions to electronic journals are more expensive, librarians want to ensure that their investment is as useful and therefore as often used as possible. The most efficient way to do this is to log the information about the journal into the library's knowledge base. The librarian enters information, such as ISSN, the library's holdings for that journal, and information about where the subscribed journal content may be found, usually a web page, into a form. Knowledge bases are covered in more detail in Chapter 7. They may also provide information required for authenticating at the destination web page. Then, when the customer searches the database or discovery service, the results list will indicate when an article is available in that local collection and, when it is available, provide a link to that title in another electronic resource. Thus, adding information about local collections using the administrative module for an electronic resource increases the chances that customers will find the full text of the article or other electronic information resource they are seeking.

Individual journal holdings are specific to each library and consist of a list of volumes and issues to which that library provides access, that is, those volumes and journals that the library has purchased and/or licensed.

CUSTOMIZING SERVICES AND PREFERENCES

The ability for a library to customize the services provided to its customers through an electronic resource interface is one of the greatest value-added elements that content providers currently provide. Web usability became a hot topic in the 2000s as the information technology industry realized that programmers are not the best judges of customers' needs when it comes to website usability. It was, they found, better to ask the people who were going to use a web page what would make it most navigable for them. See *Don't Make Me Think!* by Steve Krug (2006) for an in-depth discussion of website usability. The notions of personalization and customization as marketing tools developed rapidly during the 1990s and 2000s (Pillar 2010). Values generally held by librarians long before personalization and customization became popular marketing tools nevertheless support the idea that products (e.g., collections) and services should be selected and delivered based on the needs of the customer or the community being served by the library. It was easy for librarians to embrace the notion of personalizing and customizing the products and services they provide to the specific needs of their customers and community. Furthermore, it is entirely natural that librarians now expect to be able to customize electronic resources to their own and their customers' needs. Through a content providers' administrative module, a librarian may be able to customize the users' search experience, the display of search results, and the options for the delivery of full text, as well as to brand the resource interface with the library's colors, logo, etc.

In this context, the term "interface" is being used in the sense of graphical user interface (GUI). The *Online Dictionary of Library and Information Science* defines an interface as "The point or process that joins two components of a data processing system, for example, the screen display that functions as intermediary between a software program and its human users. Some interfaces are more user-friendly than others" (Reitz 2015).

The Search Experience

In terms of their search interfaces, content providers have paid attention to what is working for commercial sites, most prominently Google. A review of electronic resource, particularly database, search interfaces clearly reveals a move toward the use of a simplified basic search screen. Figures 6.1 through 6.5 illustrate how the front page of *JSTOR* has changed since 1998. This section will cover some of the most popular and widely used choices libraries have for customizing an electronic resource. In a discussion of customizing the search experience, it is important to remember that the details of not only what librarians can customize but also

Figure 6.1 JSTOR homepage 1998.

Source: Reprinted courtesy of JSTOR. JSTOR © 2013. All rights reserved.

how they do it will differ from content provider to content provider and sometimes from product to product. It is also important to remember that the purpose of customization of a resource for a particular population will be a decision that librarians in each library make for their own customers, hopefully based on a thorough community analysis.

Figure 6.2 JSTOR homepage 2008.

Source: Reprinted courtesy of JSTOR. JSTOR © 2013. All rights reserved.

JSTOR HOME   SEARCH ▼   BROWSE ▼   MyJSTOR ▼

Used by millions for research, teaching, and learning. With more than a thousand academic journals and over 1 million images, letters, and other primary sources, JSTOR is one of the world's most trusted sources for academic content.

SEARCH

| | SEARCH |

Advanced Search

BROWSE BY DISCIPLINE

African American Studies (17 titles)	History (262 titles)
African Studies (42 titles)	History of Science & Technology (26 titles)
American Indian Studies (6 titles)	Irish Studies (49 titles)
Anthropology (63 titles)	Jewish Studies (10 titles)
Aquatic Sciences (15 titles)	Language & Literature (242 titles)
Archaeology (62 titles)	Latin American Studies (39 titles)
Architecture & Architectural History (27 titles)	Law (73 titles)

Figure 6.3 JSTOR search page.

Source: Reprinted courtesy of JSTOR. JSTOR © 2013. All rights reserved.

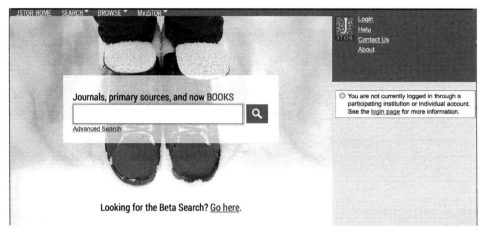

Figure 6.4 JSTOR search page.

Source: Reprinted courtesy of JSTOR. JSTOR © 2013. All rights reserved.

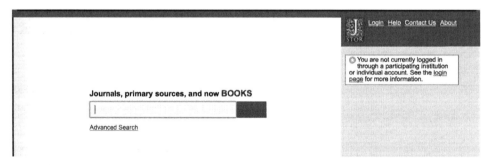

Figure 6.5 JSTOR search page.

Source: Reprinted courtesy of JSTOR. JSTOR © 2013. All rights reserved.

Most content providers currently allow librarians to select the default landing page, the web page to which the customer is directed upon choosing a link, for an electronic resource. The current trend in basic search screens is to design it so that it resembles a Google search both in appearance and in functionality. Public libraries, school libraries, and even some academic libraries serving a large undergraduate population are likely to choose the basic search screen for their customers since their customers are likely to be most familiar with conducting searches in Google. Academic libraries serving a large population of graduate students and faculty researchers are more likely to choose the advanced search screen as the landing page for electronic resources. In particular, an academic library may select the advanced search screen in electronic resources for which the primary audience is these more advanced searchers.

A basic search screen generally produces a keyword search, that is "a search of a bibliographic database in which natural language words and phrases appearing in the text of the documents indexed, or in their bibliographic descriptions, are used as search terms, rather than terms selected from a controlled vocabulary (authorized subject headings or descriptors" (Reitz 2015, sec. free-text search). Another choice a librarian may make related to the functionality of a basic search is enable or disable the display of "suggest search terms," which, when enabled, uses context and semantics to identify and display alternative search terms. The librarian may be able to choose to show or hide a link to search history, whereby the resource records the sequence of searches conducted by the customer and can display them for reference and may allow the customer to combine searches. The librarian may be able to choose to show or hide more search options on the basic search screen. More search options might include some or all of the following:

- More complex search modes like Boolean operators, application of words related to the search terms entered, and the ability to choose which parts of a document to search (e.g., abstract and full text).
- The application of limiters to results such as full text only, scholarly publications only, specific type of publication, date ranges, availability of references within an article, and images only.

A librarian may also be able to choose whether or not to display a link to an advanced search screen on the basic search screen. Figure 6.6 contains an example of the customer view of a basic search screen configured to include a basic search box, the content provider's logo, a link to the advanced search screen, a link to search history, and a list of additional search options including both more complex search modes and limiters. It also includes a link that allows customers to choose the database that they wish to search in from among those databases published by this content provider and subscribed by this library. The function may also allow the customer to search in multiple databases (databases published by this content provider and subscribed by this library) with a single search.

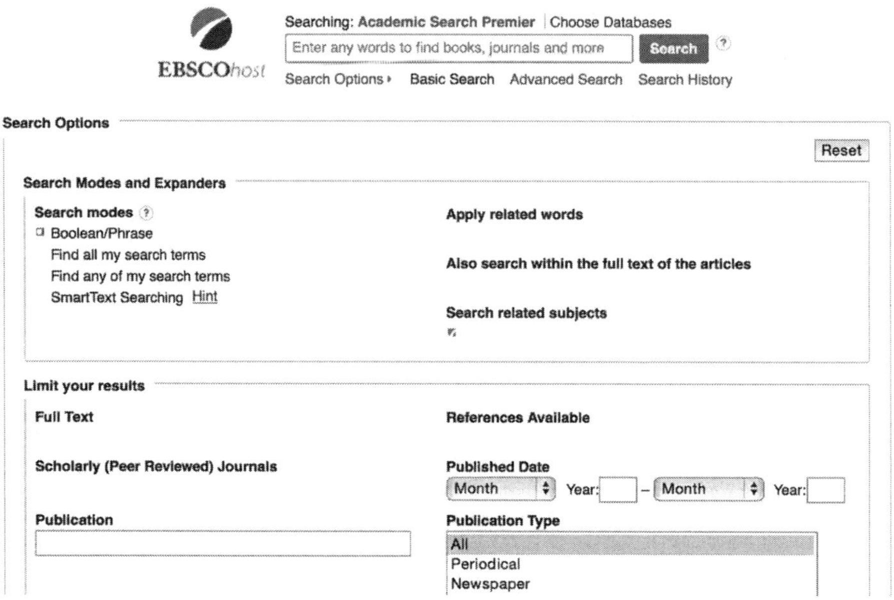

EBSCOhost

Searching: Academic Search Premier | Choose Databases

Enter any words to find books, journals and more   **Search** ?

Search Options ▸   **Basic Search**   Advanced Search   Search History

Search Options

Reset

Search Modes and Expanders

Search modes ?
- Boolean/Phrase
  Find all my search terms
  Find any of my search terms
  SmartText Searching Hint

Apply related words

Also search within the full text of the articles

Search related subjects

Limit your results

Full Text

Scholarly (Peer Reviewed) Journals

Publication

References Available

Published Date
Month ⬍ Year: ____ – Month ⬍ Year: ____

Publication Type
All
Periodical
Newspaper

Figure 6.6 EBSCO search page.

Source: Reprinted with permission.

In making choices for the basic search screen, librarians should bear in mind the fundamental purpose of a basic search screen: to reduce feelings of confusion and frustration for customers by presenting them with a limited range of choices. The more options a librarian chooses to add to a basic search screen, the less Google-like the search experience becomes. Librarians should weigh the possible benefits of additional search options to his or her customers with the customers' tolerance for complexity.

The alternative to the basic search screen is often called the advanced search screen. Here the librarian may choose to mix and match more options that will allow the more sophisticated searchers among his or her customers to create a more complex search query. Options available for customizing an advanced search screen will naturally be more elaborate than those available for customizing a basic search.

An advanced search screen usually includes multiple search boxes. In the example in Figure 6.7, you can see that this library has configured this content provider's advance search screen to include three search boxes each of which uses a drop-down menu to provide the customer with 17 fields to search. Other content providers may configure the choice of searchable fields differently, and other databases may include a different

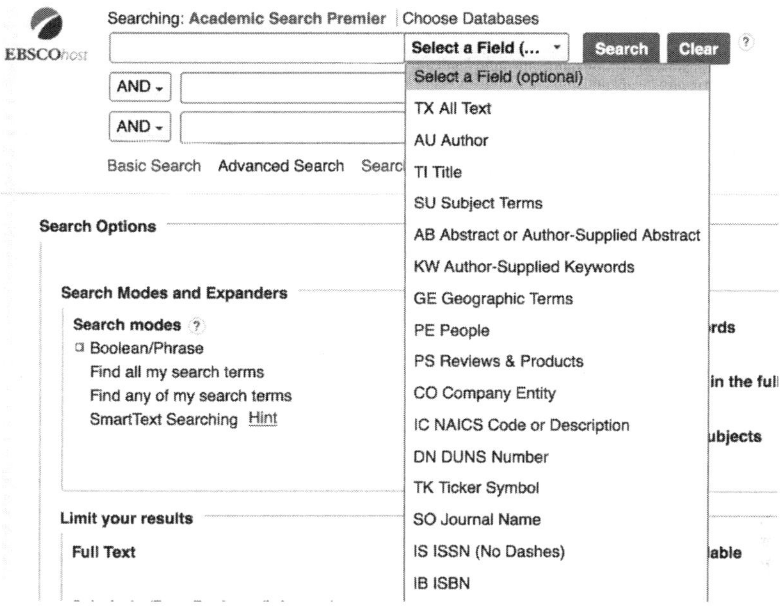

Figure 6.7 EBSCO advanced search page.
Source: Reprinted with permission.

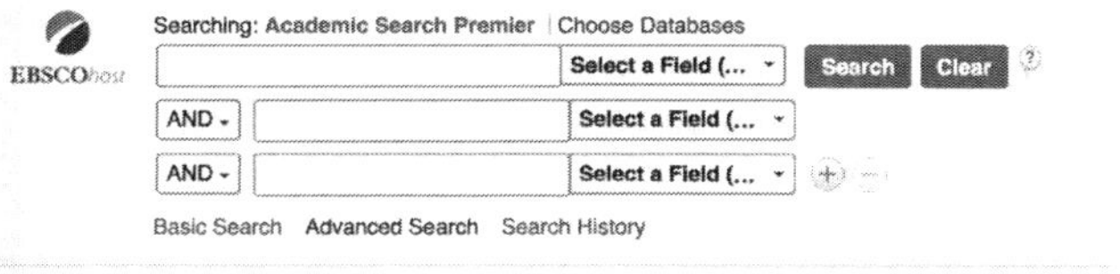

Figure 6.8 EBSCO advanced search box.
Source: Reprinted with permission.

combination of searchable field. The searchable fields available often depend on the type of document that is included in the database and/or the topic of the contents of those documents. In Figure 6.8, you can also see that this library has configured this content provider's advance search screen to allow the addition of more search boxes.

An advanced search is likely to allow Boolean searching, which is to provide a mechanism for customers to narrow their search results by including only items that have both or all of their search terms in them or to broaden their search results by including items that have just one of several search terms. An advance search screen may also include the ability to search for a string of terms in a specific order defined as phrase searching, as well as to conduct proximity searching where the customer may specify the maximum number of words separating two search terms.

An advanced search screen often includes choices for limiting the search results similar to, but often more elaborate than, those that are available for addition to a basic search screen discussed earlier. For example, in Figure 6.8, you can see that this library's configuration of this content provider's database includes the ability to limit search results based on:

- The availability of full text or the availability of full text in PDF format
- The title of a particular publication
- The type of document
- The number of pages
- A variety of image characteristics
- The language in which the document is written

Some other options that may be available for use in a basic search screen and/or an advanced search screen include session time-out, spell-checker, text-to-speech functionality, autocomplete, options for browsing thesaurus or subject terms, show suggested search terms, other more-like-this options.

Like the basic search screen, available options for customizing the user's advanced search experience will vary depending on the content provider and the resource itself. As with decisions about what to include in a basic search screen, each library should weigh the possible benefits of additional search options to its customers with its customers' tolerance for complexity.

The Results Display

Like the search experience, librarians have a wide variety of choices for customizing the display of search results to their customers. Unlike the search screen choices, there is only one results display to which options may be added or subtracted depending on the library's analysis of its customers preferences, tolerance for complexity, and search capabilities. Most electronic resources currently make use of facets in their results displays. Facets are categories of nominal properties or attributes of a document that can be used to differentiate one resource from another but which cannot be used to rank them in any particular order, for example, document X is greater than document Y (Glushko 2014, sec. Glossary). For example, subject, peer review, availability of full text, and language are all nominal facets that are often used in electronic resources. Notice that these facets are very similar to the limiters that may be made available for use in the search experience.

The results display may often be customized in appearance, that is, in the organization of information on the page. For example, a librarian may choose a page layout that makes use of one, two, or three columns. Other appearance-related choices that a librarian makes include the number of results displayed on each page, the amount of information about each result to display. This can be the title, source, excerpts of the abstract, among others, the inclusion or exclusion of clusters of results based on facets selected by the librarian, and information about the inclusion of a result in a local collection.

The results display may often be customized in functionality, defined as the options that the customer has for what they can do with results that appear in response to a search. For instance, a librarian can choose whether to automatically clear the search terms from the search boxes when the search boxes are included at the top of a results page where they often are. Other functional choices that a librarian makes include the ability to

- Select individual results from the list and save them permanently or temporarily
- Email them
- Export them to a citation management system
- Allow automatic streaming or downloading of audio and/or video content
- Choose the order in which results are displayed
- Create personalized alerts when new documents that meet the customers' criteria are added to the database
- Create a personalized free account in the database or with the content provider that would include all of that content provider's databases to which the library subscribes

The library's choices about how to customize the results display for an electronic resource should be made based on criteria similar to those on which choices about the search experience are made. But for the results display, it is also important to keep in mind that for most of the choices the library may make for the default display of results, the customer may also make on his or her own behalf. In general, any customer searching in an electronic resource may make temporary decisions about the display of search results that last only until the end of a session. But often customers may take advantage of the ability to create a free account with the resource or the content provider in which they may store their preferences for the display of search results.

Branding

The administrative module is often the place where librarians may brand the electronic resource. A librarian may decide to apply a brand to its electronic resources in order to create a more seamless searching experience for its customers across multiple resources. This purpose is based on the librarian's position as expert, for having vetted resources for customer use; it is meant to increase the customers' confidence that the information they find will be trustworthy. A librarian may also decide to apply a brand to its electronic resources in order to communicate to its customers the financial value that the library has invested in the resource. Branding also provides a means for the user to hyperlink back to a library's website.

As with some of the other functions available in the administrative module, branding options will vary slightly between different content providers. Most content providers, however, will make some or all of the following options available: the ability to change the color scheme of the electronic resource interface, the ability to insert messages and links, for example, to an Ask-A-Librarian service, the ability to use the library's logo in the interface, and the ability to adjust content in the page header and footer for some or all of interface pages. The level of technological expertise required to brand an interface will also vary from content provider to content provider. Knowledge of basic HTML and CSS will be very helpful to a librarian working on branding an electronic resource interface. Many content providers also provide support for branding in the form of best practices and/or customer service agents to help with some or all of the process.

Other Customization Options

Different content providers may offer additional customization options to their library clients. One popular option is often used in situations where the library subscribes to multiple databases from a single content provider in support of the needs of several disparate groups of customer. This option, sometimes called create groups or create profiles, gives librarians the ability to create groups of users for whom the collections can be customized with some but not all of the subscribed electronic resources. For example, academic librarians might create separate groups or profiles for undergraduate students and graduate students in specific disciplines. A collection of electronic resources for undergraduate students might include a multidisciplinary or general topics database, a collection of encyclopedias, and a database offering multiple perspectives on current issues of the day. It would probably also use the basic search screens as the entry points since undergraduate students are often unsophisticated searchers who will be comfortable with a Google-like search interface.

In addition to providing the library's customers with alerting services, for example, receiving an email containing the table of contents of a newly published journal issue, many content providers provide librarians with alerting services to inform them of new products, new features added to existing products, changes and upgrades to existing products, and new training opportunities. Training opportunities offered by content providers are an excellent means for librarians and library staff to keep up to date not only with the features of electronic resource products that will be of interest to library customers, but also with the features available to library staff for improving the customer experience.

PROXY SERVERS AND AUTHENTICATION

Another very important use of a content provider's administrative module is for controlling access to the library's subscribed resources. Recall the discussion at the beginning of this chapter and in Chapter 5. Electronic resources are often governed by a license agreement that, among other things, restricts the use of the resource to library customers. This restriction usually describes the library's customers in a way that excludes people who are not affiliated with the specific institutions, and it almost always puts the onus on the library staff to enforce this restriction. What this means in terms of providing access to library-subscribed electronic resources is that the librarian must find a way to provide access only to authorized users, which is often done using authentication and proxy servers.

In the context of electronic resources in libraries, authentication is "the process of validating an assertion of identity" (Millman 2009, 413) by a library customer in order to gain access to a proprietary, subscribed electronic resource. Libraries should first ensure that the computers and other devices linking to the Internet within their institution be registered with their content providers. As before, this can be accomplished through the administrative module. The subscribing institution, that is, the library and other facilities within the larger organization, such as classrooms, will have a range of IP addresses associated with its computing devices. This range should be registered with each content provider.

An IP address is "the physical address of a client or server computer attached to a network governed by the TCP/IP protocol, written as four sets of Arabic numerals separated by dots (*example*: 123.456.78.9)" (Reitz 2015). IP addresses are sometimes static, that is, assigned permanently to a particular computer. But more often, they are dynamic, meaning that they are "owned" by a particular entity, like the library, and so permanently and uniquely assigned to the library. However, within the library's network, they are assigned uniquely but temporarily to a particular computer. The computer to which a dynamic IP address is assigned may be hardwired as in a library staff member's desktop workstation or wirelessly as in a library patron using the library's wireless network connected to the library's network. Dynamic IP addresses are usually considered more cost efficient since they may be reused by multiple library customers and/or staff members one at a time. This means that the library needs to pay for a smaller number of IP addresses.

During the process of implementing a new licensed electronic resource, library staff will enter the range of IP addresses assigned to their network in a section of the content provider's administrative module. It is important that this be done exactly in the way the administrative module describes. A range of IP addresses may be expressed in several ways, for example,

- 123.456.789.001 through 123.456.793.999
- 123.456.789.001–123.456.793.999
- 123.456.789.* through 123.45.6.793.*
- 123.456.789.*–123.456.789.*

are all ways to express IP addresses.

Recall the discussion at the beginning of this chapter and in the chapter about the rules governing the use of a subscribed resource. Electronic resources are often governed by a license agreement that, among other things, restricts the use of the resource to library customers. As stated earlier in this chapter, this restriction usually describes the library's customers in a way that excludes people who are not affiliated with the specific institutions, and it almost always puts the onus on the library staff to enforce this restriction. What this means in terms of providing access to library-subscribed electronic resources is that the librarian must find a way to provide access only to authorized users. Since not all library customers access resources from within the organization's IP range, the library must make use of authentication and proxy servers. Library customers using a computer or device assigned an IP address within the institutional range will be able to seamlessly access the digital content licensed by the library, provided that the IP range has been correctly added to the content provider's administration module. This is known as local access. If however, the library customer is working from home or the coffee shop up the street, the device connecting them to the Internet will not have an IP address within the library's range. This is known as remote use and requires that the customer authenticate their identity as a legitimate library customer before proceeding to use the resource. Authentication may take place in a number of ways. The least preferable alternative is providing the end user with a username/password combination; these are easily shared with non-authorized users. Single sign-on services, such as the open-source Shibboleth software, offer libraries a means of authenticating remote users. Another popular option is to implement a proxy server.

All resources available through remote access require that the library authenticate remote users through an authentication service, such as Shibboleth or a proxy server, such as EZ Proxy. A proxy server is "an application program that operates between a client and server on a computer network, usually installed as a firewall to provide security, such as checking authentication" (Reitz 2015). Proxy servers are installed on a device with an IP address within the institution's range and so are recognized by the content provider once the user has been authenticated and the request for a resource is forwarded. In libraries and other information agencies, a proxy server is usually implemented in order to comply with a content provider's requirement to restrict access to a licensed electronic resource.

PUTTING IT ALL TOGETHER

The Customer's View

When library customers select a link to a subscribed electronic resource like a database from the library's web page, what happens next depends on where they and their device are physically located. If they are local, that is, using a computer that is in the library's network and therefore assigned an IP address within the library's owned range, the customer will see displayed the default landing page for the resource, the one that the library has selected and customized in the resource's administrative module. From there, the customer may begin to search the resource. If they are remote, that is using a computer that is outside the library's network and therefore using an IP address outside the library's owned range, the customers will see displayed a log-in screen where they must enter credentials such as their library card number and password. Once their log-in is accepted, then they will see displayed the default landing page for the resource. Notice that when an IP address is used for authentication on a computer inside the library's network, the authentication transaction is nearly invisible to the customer.

The Internal Operations

What happens behind the scenes, invisible or nearly so from the customer's view, when the library customer selects a link to a subscribed electronic resource like a database from the library's web page, is a more complex set of operations. When the library customer selects a link to a licensed electronic resource like a database from the library's web page using a computer that is in the library's network, it is not necessary for an authentication request to be sent to the proxy server. However, to facilitate dynamic linking through the knowledge base, a proxy server prefix is often routed with every request. Because the customer's computer is using an IP address in the range of IP addresses assigned to the library's network (including the proxy server's IP address), it is recognized as authorized, and the request is granted with no further interaction with the customer. The proxy server alerts the resource that the request is from an authorized user, and the resource accepts the request for access and displays the default landing page on its site.

When the library customer selects a link to a subscribed electronic resource like a database from the library's web page using a computer that is external to the library's network, a request for authentication is sent to the proxy server. Since the customer's computer is using an IP address outside the range of IP addresses assigned to the library's network, it is not recognized, and the customer must provide credentials identifying themselves as an authorized user. The proxy server directs the user's computer to display a log-in screen. If the customer enters acceptable credentials, the proxy server alerts the resource that the request is from an authorized user, and the resource accepts the request for access and displays the default landing page on its site. If not, the user is denied access to the resource.

Single Sign-On Services

In providing information resource and services to customers, libraries and information agencies operate, and often operate within, a variety of independent systems. For example, an academic library operates its own systems such as an integrated library system (ILS), online catalog, and subscribed electronic resources. But it also operates within the systems of the entity of which it is a part, the college or university. The library's systems must interact with the college or university's systems, for example, the library's ILS must be able to communicate with the university's student information and human resources systems in order to obtain lists of current students, faculty, and staff. In order to facilitate such communication and to reduce the number of times users of these systems must authenticate themselves not to mention keep track of usernames and password for each one, some institutions use a single sign-on service. A single sign-on service allows users to negotiate all or most of an institution's systems using a single credential. Further, it limits the number of user accounts that systems administrators must manage and track. In libraries and other information agencies, single sign-on services like Shibboleth and Athens allow users to access all types of library resources and services, for example, interlibrary load, electronic resources, and institutional repositories, through a single authentication.

TECHNOLOGICAL EXPERTISE

The preceding explanations are simplified versions of a much more complex process. One of the things that make them complex is that the process of communication between the proxy server and the subscribed resource, while following the same general process, may vary slightly but significantly from content provider to content provider. Small variances can make the difference between smooth authentication and denied access, which can cause library customers and staff considerable frustration. EZProxy, a leading proxy server currently used in many libraries, makes use of a listserv where updates are posted for configuring library resource proxies.

Another complexity that is not explored in depth here is the technologies that underlie authentication and proxy servers. As has been depicted in this chapter, some technological expertise beyond that of a generalist librarian is required to manage electronic resources and authentication. But what is required can be compared with the technological expertise required to drive a car. A driver must have knowledge of some specific terminology and the way the controls of a car will function but does not necessarily need to have in-depth knowledge of internal combustion engines in order to drive the car. Similarly, a librarian with the responsibility for managing electronic resources must have knowledge of some specific terminology and the way the content providers' administrative modules will function, but does not need the expert knowledge of a computer scientist or programmer in order to operate the administrative modules.

ACTIVITIES

1. [Administrative modules] Choose a proprietary electronic resource/database to which your library subscribes, identify the vendor or publisher, then explore the content provider's website. Look for the section of the website that is written for librarians, specifically, look for any guides, instruction, help sheets, or tutorials the content provider provides. Browse through these materials and then go back to your library's version of the resource. What kinds of customization has your library done to the resource's interface? Why do you think it made the choices it made? What might you change about its choices and why?
2. Take the tutorial on EZProxy at https://www.oclc.org/support/training/portfolios/electronic-collection-management/ezproxy/tutorials/ezproxy-overview.en.html.

REFERENCES

Bade, David W. 2007. "Structures, Standards, and the People Who Make Them Meaningful." In Library of Congress. Retrieved from http://www.loc.gov/bibliographic-future/meetings/docs/bade-may9-2007.pdf.

Glushko, R.J. 2014. *The Discipline of Organizing: Professional Edition*. O'Reilly Media.

Krug, Steve. 2006. *Don't Make Me Think!: A Common Sense Approach to Web Usability*. Berkeley, CA: New Riders.

Millman, David. 2009. "Authentication and Authorization." In *Encyclopedia of Library and Information Sciences, Third Edition*, 413–19. Taylor & Francis.

Pillar, Frank. 2010. "Mass Customization, Customer Integration, Open Innovation & Personalization." Retrieved from http://www.iimcp.org/.

Reitz, Joan. 2015. *ODLIS: Online Dictionary of Library and Information Science.* Retrieved from http://lu.com/odlis/search.cfm.

FURTHER READING

Millman, D. 2009. "Authentication and Authorization." In *Encyclopedia of Library and Information Sciences*, Third Edition, 413–19. Taylor & Francis.

OCLC. 2015. "OCLC EZproxy: An Overview." Retrieved June 12, 2015, from https://www.oclc.org/support/training/portfolios/electronic-collection-management/ezproxy/tutorials/ezproxy-overview.en.en.html.

The Open Group. 2010. "Introduction to Single Sign-On." Retrieved June 13, 2015, from http://www.opengroup.org/security/sso/sso_intro.htm.

Chapter 7
Managing Access and Discovery

Electronic resource librarians spend their days working with the products and services licensed to them by their content providers. It is important that electronic resource librarians maintain daily engagement with their colleagues in the vendor and publisher sectors, as well as other electronic resource librarians, either directly or indirectly. At their institutions, they are expected to be the experts in all things digital. They cannot have content expertise in all of the library's resources; however, they should be very familiar with changes in the content. They must know the search and retrieval functionality of the databases forward and backward. Other librarians in the institution will turn to the electronic resource librarian for guidance. Once the resources are properly configured for discovery and access and their accompanying metadata has been captured and stored, the electronic resource librarian can focus on the tasks of everyday management of the resources. Ensuring that the library customer has a fruitful and seamless experience is not always an easy task. There are several points in the flow of data from the search request to the delivery of full text where something can go wrong. Usually, there is a change external to the library that has not been communicated to the electronic resource librarian, and so the local integrated systems have not been configured to accommodate the change. Other discovery and access issues may occur because an internal configuration that seemed to be functional was discovered by a user to have an unintended flaw. Try as they may, electronic resource librarians cannot foresee all possible consequences of their actions.

Environmental scanning involves careful monitoring of the library, its needs and its resources, and its external environment. The electronic resource librarian should be aware of opportunities and threats that may influence the library's digital environment.

The internal systems under the control of the electronic resource librarian are a complex of integrated modules. These modules are often proprietary, though some larger libraries with the appropriate staff will build their own systems or employ an open-source option. Of the many proprietary offerings, libraries can opt to host the software locally, which allows for greater control. Alternately, librarians may choose to have the software hosted by the content provider, in which case the electronic resource librarian will perform the management functions remotely through a web interface. It is essential for electronic resource librarians to understand these systems, the standards that underpin their functioning, and how they work together to provide the best possible end-user experience.

SYSTEMS

At the center of the library's systems for managing electronic resources is the knowledge base. The knowledge base holds all of the information about the library's digital collections that enables the smooth discovery and delivery of resources to the end user. It is a centralized data repository that includes:

- Information about journals, books, conference proceedings, and other types of scholarly materials
- Descriptive metadata
- Peer-review indicators
- Information about journal and book collections and packages, both subscription based and open access
- Indexing that covers individual journals within the collections and packages (year, volume, and issue)

- Full text that covers individual journals within the collections and packages (year, volume, and issue)
- Indication of any "moving wall" gaps
- Configurations tools
- Citation-downloading tools
- Linking to OPACs
- Linking to document delivery forms
- Locally managed services and scholarly materials
- Custom holdings information
- Institutional repository

Ensuring that the information in the library's knowledge base is correct and current is very important. Fortunately, knowledge base vendors offer updating services releasing the librarian from what would arguably be the full-time work of several people. This is so because the titles and the coverage of those titles within any given collection or package are continually in flux. The library licenses the use of a collection for a certain period of time. The content provider hosting that collection will have, in turn, licenses with the various publishers providing titles to be included in the collection. The agreements between the content provider and publishers will invariably change over the course of the library's subscription period. Changes in the titles and holdings associated with a package are expected. Often, these changes occur with little notice by the user community as there is usually redundancy in journal title holdings. However, the more high–profile changes, such as a change in an exclusive license between a publisher and a content provider, will be announced and receive attention on listservs and blogs.

Before the advent of the automatically updated knowledge base, keeping up with title changes was a daunting task. Early electronic resource librarians would spend untold hours trying to update records and fix broken links. In 1999, a clever and enterprising reference librarian, Peter McCracken from the University of Washington's Odegaard Undergraduate Library, with the help of colleagues, developed a solution to this serials conundrum called Serials Solutions. The idea was to create one central database with all of the updated title and holdings data for the available journal and eBook packages. Subscribers to the service would submit a profile of the library's electronic resource subscriptions and periodically receive an updated list of titles to match the profile.

This was an efficient solution welcomed by all electronic resource librarians and arguably the impetus for today's knowledge base. Initially, the fledgling company would send to its subscribers a set of html documents and a style sheet each month. The electronic resource librarian would have to manually change out the html pages on the library's website. Catalog records, if they were being kept for electronic resources, would also need to be changed. After a time, the files were delivered in xml. Eventually, Serials Solutions offered a hosted alternative, releasing the electronic resource librarian from the task of monthly updates. This change also had the benefit of providing instantaneous updates. Together, these files made up the initial A–Z list of journals that the library subscribes to; the list was one of the first devices used for discovering electronic resources outside of the online catalog. While A–Z lists of journals continue to be offered, the titles will more likely be generated directly from the library's knowledge base.

While the journal A–Z list was a welcome finding tool for library users, it was often confusing for them and for librarians to determine how to get from an indexing record that contained only metadata about a resource to the full text of that resource. Indexing databases were very common and often offered as a stand-alone resource. Academic researchers valued and understood indexes. It was natural that these resources were the first to be digitized. In the days of print, it was understood that once a desired citation was found, the next step was to find the journal on the shelf. With the appearance of online full text, finding the desired article could be quite cumbersome. It required returning to the library's website, finding the journal in the title list, selecting from the available subscription options while ensuring that the date of the desired article falls within the listed holdings date, entering the databases that should have the article, and searching for, finding and downloading the article.

Even when this process was followed correctly, the searcher would often still encounter problems. Despite the best efforts of electronic resource librarians to keep their title lists up to date, the titles and holdings reported by content providers were often erroneous or misleading. For instance, Journal Title A might be reported as having full-text coverage for 2001. This coverage, however, may extend only to February 2001 or perhaps there are only two articles from Journal Title A from 2001. A notable case, *New York Times Co. v. Tasini*, 533 U.S. 483 (2001), determined that publishers could not license the works of freelance journalists contained in the newspapers to electronic database vendors. This resulted in the sudden disappearance of many articles. If there was just one full-text article for a given years, content providers would still report having the full text for that year. Library users would often hit dead ends trying to find full text. These coverage discrepancies still occur today; however, the path to the dead-end result is much shorter and straighter thanks to the development of inter-database linking.

Content providers were experimenting with cross-database linking as soon as full text became available. Content providers would have agreements with each other to provide linking from a given indexing database to a full-text database. The technologies employed in this linking were proprietary and unique to the partners to the deals. If electronic resource librarians desired to take advantage of these improvements, they would need to configure the library's subscription resources through each of the administrative modules to link out or receive links to various other resources. Every time a linking agreement changed, so did these configurations. Sometimes changes in linking agreements were not communicated to library customers until the very last minute or at all. This, of course, led to broken links to the full-text resource.

When hitting a dead end from a direct link, users often assumed that it had been their only option for finding that particular resource. This was usually not the case, however. If the user had not been given a direct link, they would have consulted the A–Z list to determine which databases might have their article of interest. All of the possible points of access to a copy of the article would be presented. While the previous long path to the full text was more cumbersome, at least end users were presented with all of the various full-text options and could redirect their journey through a different database. The front-runner in the evolution of direct linking from a metadata record in one database to a full-text resource was the integrated library system vendor ExLibris. Early work by Herbert Van de Sompel, a librarian at the University of Ghent resulted in a product called SFX, which was acquired and promoted by ExLibris. A National Information Standards Organization (NISO) working group convened in 2001 to develop an open standard to facilitate direct linking among electronic resource databases, called OpenURL. This was a sensitive time for vendors and platform developers who were investing considerably in such technologies. While wishing to protect their investments and their exclusive relationships, they also recognized that interoperability among the players in the information environment would require an open standard. Many vendors were represented on the working group to guard their interests. Two years into development, something happened that alarmed the committee and disrupted progress for a short while.

In her white paper on "Patents and Open Standards," Priscilla Caplan (2003), describes the event as if it were a matter of course. However, listservs at the time were abuzz with fearful and angry commentary. NISO learned that a patent had been filed by one of the committee members, Eric Hellman, president of Openly Informatics. The NISO board appointed a committee to determine whether content providers using OpenURL would infringe upon the patent if it were granted. The committee determined that yes, "with broad interpretation, implementers of OpenURL resolvers will infringe upon the patent." Hellman, caught in a tight spot, granted a no-cost license for the patented technology to NISO and its members for the purposes of implementing link-resolver software. There continued to be disquiet about the situation among content providers as it was possible that after developing and implementing OpenURL technologies in libraries the world over, another party may acquire this patent and require a fee for every instance of linking. This cost, of course, would be passed along to the libraries. This has not happened. OCLC is the current maintenance organization for the OpenURL standard.

STANDARDS

In order for these various systems to be effective, all organizations in the information supply chain need to be on the same page. That is, they need to use the same type of metadata, formatted in the same way and exchanged using the same protocols. Without standardization, knowledge bases cannot be effectively populated and links between resources will not be resolved. A cluster of standards have evolved to improve the user search and retrieval experience: OpenURL Z39.88, Knowledge Base and Related Tools (KBART), and Improving OpenURLs through Analytics (IOTA).

As mentioned previously, work on the OpenURL standard began in the early 2000s. In 2004, the NISO working group published ANSI/NISO Z39.88–2004 The OpenURL Framework for Context-Sensitive Services. This standard was revised in 2010. It defines architecture for creating OpenURL Framework Applications, which is a networked service environment that exchanges packages of information. These packages contain the metadata about an information resource used as well as information about the contextual networked environments so that parties to the linking can be identified and the requests and responses can be transferred effectively. The standard refers to the information packages as ContextObjects and sets out definitions for the complex of components they contain. It also defines what it calls Transport, which is a mechanism that enables communities to specify how to transport ContextObject representations. Lastly, the standard specifies how to "deploy a new OpenURL Framework Application by defining a new Community Profile" (NISO 2010).

The early implementation of OpenURL was relatively simple in concept in that it used standard HTTP commands to transfer information about an information resource from an information provider to a linking server and vice versa. A URL is constructed initially when a user finds a metadata record for resource of interest and initiates a request. This metadata record is called the source; it provides information about the resource and the library's link resolver. When the link resolver receives the OpenURL, it consults the knowledge base and constructs a URL that identifies full-text alternatives called targets. These results are then delivered to the user that initiated the request. The following is an example of an OpenURL adapted from the NISO website.

```
http://www.example.com/resolver?genre=article
&atitle=OpenURL Standards Rock
&title=Libraries Today
&aulast=Librarian
&aufirst=Harrison
&date=2015
&volume=10
&issue=1
&spage=10
&epage=15
```

Because of its core simplicity, developers were able to quickly produce products that could use the standard. The committee recognized the status of this early version of OpenURL as a "de facto standard" (NISO 2010). The OpenURL Framework Standard (Z39.88–2004) refers to the early version as OpenURL 0.1, and the OpenURL 0.1 specifications are retained in the OpenURL Framework Registry at http://www.openurl.info/registry/docs/pdf/openurl-01.pdf. The committee put in place a simple protocol for extensibility to allow for more complexity in description and the transmission of data. The current standard is a 104-page document and is considerably more complex than set out earlier.

After several years of using link resolvers, librarians and others in the information supply chain recognized more standards work needed to be done if the technology was going to perform as efficiently and effectively as it was intended. In the late 2000s, a working group convened to identify interoperability issues and recommend solutions. In 2010, the NISO RP-9–2010 KBART was released. This recommended practice was revised and republished in 2014 to accommodate emerging digital formats and complex institutional relationships. The purpose of both versions is to provide guidance to all parties in the information supply chain regarding "the role of metadata within the OpenURL linking standard, and recommends data formatting and exchange guidelines for publishers, aggregators, agents, technology vendors, and librarians to adhere to when exchanging information about their respective content holdings for use in knowledge bases, also called link resolvers" (NISO 2014).

In 2010, a new working group was formed to aid information providers who want to improve the quality of their metadata, by helping them pinpoint problem areas. This committee was charged with designing a systematic method to benchmark the quality of data supplied by information providers to be used by OpenURL link resolvers. The problem statement notes that too often these links do not work as expected, leaving users with a less-than-desired quality of service. They developed what they call a Completeness Index as a method of predicting the success of OpenURL linking from a given information provider through the examination of the data elements provided by their site. The Completeness Index and Completeness Score are sensitive to various contextual factors within the linking environment, such as the ability of a link resolver to handle more or less granular metadata, and its ability to automatically enhance metadata by matching it with external data that might aid in identification and disambiguation.

After three years of research and testing, NISO approved and released the recommended practice in 2013 called NISO RP-21–2013 Improving OpenURLs through Analytics (IOTA): Recommendations for Link Resolver Providers. They anticipate that by "applying this Completeness

Index to their OpenURL data and following the recommendations, providers of link resolvers can monitor the quality of their OpenURLs and work with content providers to improve the provided metadata ultimately resulting in a higher success rate for end users" (NISO 2013).

DISCOVERY

By 2003, nearly every academic library was equipped with a knowledge base and an OpenURL link resolver. While there were still issues to be resolved with these systems, librarians had set their sights on improving the search experience for users. Library users were becoming accustomed to a more streamlined process of information retrieval. Internet search engines had simplified searching to typing in keywords to a single search box to retrieve all of the indexed pages available on the World Wide Web. This was a very different model from what was available through the library and its various resources. Keyword searching was considered by librarians to be an inferior method for retrieving optimum precision and recall from a query and so default search forms tended to offer and encourage more advanced searching. Another big difference between the user's library's experience and an Internet search engine experience was the inability to search all available records in one fell swoop. The first attempt to solve these discrepancies in user experience was the adoption of federated searching.

A federated search is a technology that facilitates a simultaneous search of multiple databases. A query is entered by a user from one location and that query is then automatically sent out to all of the electronic databases designated by the electronic resource librarian. The databases retrieve the relevant records and push them back to the library's federated search tool. The software then compiles the results and delivers them to the user. Initially, this seemed like a great idea. Not long after widespread implementation, however, librarians and content providers alike were ready to try something different. This technology comes with all of the advantages of Internet search engines and also comes with some of its disadvantages. For instance, the number of results is overwhelming and ultimately does not improve the result for the end user. First of all, they forego the ability to select the most relevant databases for their subject area. To get around this, electronic resource librarians could set up custom federated searches for a topic area that would only query selected resources. This certainly improves the relevance of the results; however, the sheer number of relevant results is too overwhelming for a researcher or student.

As we continue to see today, only the results at the top of the list tend to be consulted. This can be expected. Even a typical search on a single database retrieves more results than that can ever be manageable in a single setting. That is why databases are usually set to default sort by relevance. If an end user is going to use only the first 10 results, at least they will be the most relevant 10 results. The problem with the federated results is that once results were returned to the library's federated search tool by the databases, there was no effective way to integrate them and sort the whole set by relevance. Each content provider platform has its own proprietary algorithm for sorting relevance. In order to combine results and resort, there needed to be some transparency by the content providers, if not with their ranking mechanisms, then with the metadata used for the purposes of ranking.

This kind of cooperation was not going to come to pass. The result was a stacking of results, the order of which could be determined by the electronic resource librarian. For instance, a search retrieved 100 results each from three databases. Results 1–100 would be for Database A, results 101–200 would be from Database B, and so on. If a database was not stacked on top, those results would likely never get seen by the searcher. Making matters worse, every time a searcher sent a query from a federated search box, it would ping the servers of the databases included in the library's set. Content providers were being inundated with search queries and receiving few, if any, actual requests for resources. Federated search was a suboptimal tool for all parties in the library information supply chain.

Why did Internet search engines provide such a good experience when the library's federated search tool failed? First, the Internet does not conduct a simultaneous search on all possible web resources each time a search is conducted. Second, an Internet search engine has the ability to harvest metadata from the available resources and manipulate it in such a way to deliver results that present the most relevant options first. These two things are accomplished by web crawlers that harvest metadata and pull it together into a single index. A sorting algorithm is applied to the index based on the user's query, serving up the best results. Vendors adopted this strategy and dubbed the technology as a discovery tool or discovery layer.

Discovery tools have since evolved to search not only the library's digital resources, but also the catalog of print resources, open-access resources, etc. The move seems to be toward searching not only across all subject areas, but also across all formats. Discovery tools work on principles similar to those that work so well for Internet search engines. Rather than conducting simultaneous searches in the native interfaces of multiple databases, discovery tools search a pre-indexed (and regularly updated) knowledge base customized to each individual library's holdings. This allows discovery tool search results to be relevance ranked according to the discovery tool's algorithms rather than those of each native database. Discovery layer searching also results in a speedier search and results display than was possible with federated searches.

Discovery tools also have some disadvantages. They can be expensive; this was particularly true when they were first introduced in the market. Creating and maintaining a customized index/knowledge base for each library client is expensive, and that expense was passed along to libraries. In 2012, a medium-sized academic library with roughly 1 million owned items and 250 electronic database subscriptions would have paid about $35,000 annually for a discovery tool that indexed its catalog and all of its databases. A discovery tool adds yet another system to the layers of systems that the electronic resource librarian must manage. More complexity seldom leads to fewer issues that require troubleshooting. Discovery tools' interfaces are currently designed to resemble the ubiquitous Google search box, which is arguably comfortable for customers but itself presents challenges for the electronic resource librarian. First and foremost, because it looks like Google, customers assume that it will work like Google, keyword searching "everything" on the web. However, on balance, most librarians agree that discovery tools provide great benefit to their customers.

Managing access and discovery requires that the electronic resource librarian be knowledgeable about the systems and standards that have coevolved over the past 15 years to support the best possible user experience. This knowledge can be tapped when troubleshooting access problems, participating on a vendor focus group, or sitting on a standards committee. These are the kinds of activities that electronic resource librarians engage in on an ongoing basis. This knowledge is also indispensable when evaluating content and software products. New products are continually entering the market. The ongoing assessment of the market and the libraries' subscriptions are the topics of Chapter 8.

ACTIVITY

1. The vendor, ExLibris, now offers a product called Alma, which it claims will "unify the disparate systems today's libraries manage for electronic, digital, and print resources; optimize workflows through shared data and collaborative services as well as a cloud-based infrastructure; and re-direct resources to focus on extending library services within and outside their institutions in direct support of teaching and research goals." Read more at http://www.exlibrispublications.com/alma/. The vendor promotes the unification of resources, optimization of workflows, and redirection of resources to be improvements. What might be considered disadvantages of this system, from the librarian's perspective and from the end-user's perspective?

REFERENCES

Caplan, P. 2003. "Patents and Open Standards." Baltimore: National Information Standards Organization. Retrieved from http://www.niso.org/publications/white_papers/Patents_Caplan.pdf.

National Information Standards Organization. 2010. "ANSI/NISO Z39.88–2004 (R2010) The OpenURL Framework for Context-Sensitive Services." Baltimore: National Information Standards Organization. Retrieved from http://www.niso.org/apps/group_public/project/details.php?project_id=82.

National Information Standards Organization. 2013. "NISO RP-21–2013 Improving OpenURLs through Analytics (IOTA): Recommendations for Link Resolver Providers." Baltimore: National Information Standards Organization. Retrieved from http://www.niso.org/apps/group_public/project/details.php?project_id=115.

National Information Standards Organization. 2014. "NISO RP-9–2014 Knowledge Base and Related Tools (KBART)." Baltimore: National Information Standards Organization. Retrieved from http://www.niso.org/apps/group_public/project/details.php?project_id=122.

FURTHER READING

Hellman, E. 2003. "Open Letter to NISO." Bloomfield, NJ: Openly Informatics. Retrieved from http://www.openly.com/company/linkbatonpatent.html.

Chapter 8
Assessing Electronic Resources

Electronic resource management is an ongoing iterative process, requiring persistent attention from the electronic resource librarian. Surveying the information environment for new products, shifts in supplier relationships, feedback from the community of practice about content provider service, developments in recommended practices, and impactful policies, among other things, is a daily aspect of the job. Managing access and troubleshooting problems that surface around access at multiple points in the data stream between end user and resource provider is another attribute of the job that may require daily attention as well. While it is important to allow time to attend to these important aspects of electronic resource management, the exact issues and the amount of time that may be required to handle them cannot be predicted. However, the area of assessment is a part of electronic resource management that can and should be planned.

Emery and Stone (2013a), in their piece on conducting annual reviews, emphasize the importance of ongoing evaluation and assessment of resources. It is essential not only to ensure the fiscal well-being of the library, but also to maintain resources that are current and relevant to the library's user community (Emery and Stone 2013a). Given the importance of digital resources in today's library, it is not surprising that this has become an increasingly important part of the work of an electronic resource librarian.

Evaluating and communicating the value of a resource requires a facility for critical thinking and interpersonal skills. It also requires a plan. All resources and services should be on an evaluation schedule, and reports to various interested parties should be scheduled so that they can inform decision making at critical points.

ASSESSMENT PLANNING

While it may seem that much of the assessment and reporting work would take place just before the end of a budgeting cycle, and it often does, it is good practice to pace the assessment more evenly throughout the year so that the electronic resource librarian does not have to oversee the collection and assimilation of a year's worth of raw data and his or her colleagues who review the reports aren't overwhelmed with too much information at once. Creating an assessment schedule that staggers assessment tasks over the year is a useful strategy for reducing assessment fatigue. It may also assist in pinpointing resources that may be underutilized in a timelier manner; this allows for more space to identify and explore the problem and possible solutions or alternatives.

Every licensed resource should be evaluated every year; this includes discovery records for demand-driven plans. This may seem a daunting task at first, but with sound planning and a protocol for evaluation that prevents scope creep, this can be easily achieved. Emery and Stone suggest beginning by first dividing your fiscal year into quarters. Then, assign subscriptions to a particular quarter based on their renewal date. The review should take place at least three months prior to the end of the current license (Emery and Stone 2013a). This is necessary because some content providers will begin the renewal process months in advance of the end of the current license. Similarly, if there is a decision to NOT renew the license, the library will want to announce this decision before the cutoff date agreed upon in the license cancellation clause.

All of these dates should be recorded in your electronic resource management system (ERMS) or local administrative metadata database. Simply sort the resources and assign a quarter for review. It may be that some of the resources will be reviewed several months before a renewal or non-renewal needs to be communicated. This may be necessary to even out the workload over the course of a year. However, at least a year's worth of use data should be available for a fair evaluation of the resource. Some electronic resource librarians will purposefully have license renewals fall within the same month so that a complete evaluation can take place at once. This may be useful if there is a particular time of year that is typically slower, during which you can completely devote yourself to the task, for example, summers in a traditional academic library.

Once a schedule is in place, the electronic resource librarian and the database assessment team will want to determine which metrics will be most useful to inform decision making. It is no longer sufficient for electronic resource librarians to gather and compile raw data for reference staff and subject liaisons to pore over; there are just too many resources and too many possible metrics. It is the responsibility of the electronic resource librarian to create meaningful reports that distill information about the resources, their value, and their limitations. This requires attention to license details, usage, customer service, comparable products, and institutional requirements. The electronic resource librarian adds value to this compiled data for the purpose of sound, informed decision making. Aside from ensuring seamless access, assessing electronic resources is arguably the most important aspects of an electronic resource librarian position.

The exact areas that may be considered more or less essential to the assessment process will be determined by the library, its institutional culture, and its fiscal constraints, among other things. At minimum, the electronic resource librarian should collect data on changes in the needs of the user community, resource use, license and pricing changes, changes in titles and coverage, and content provider performance. Unless the resource is new to the library, there should already be a file with historical assessment information. Use data, reports, and decision-making records from previous cycles. Use this as a base and record changes that have taken place during the cycle under review.

- Community profile
  - Who uses the resource and why?
  - What format of it is most useful for these users?
  - Is this resource essential (e.g., accreditation, cooperative collection development agreement)?
  - Which titles within the resource are essential?
  - Would an equivalent substitute product be acceptable?
  - Does the user community receive regular instruction on the resource?

- Resource profile
  - Which titles are included?
  - What is the indexing and full-text coverage for each title?
  - Is there significant overlap of titles with other resources?
  - Are there important titles offered exclusively through this resource?
  - What is the influence of exclusive tiles through impact factor or Eigenfactor?
  - Is there an equivalent substitute resource?
- Content provider profile
  - Are the library staff and user community satisfied with the content provider platform?
  - Are there barriers to use due to digital rights management software?
  - Does the content provider provide seamless access between the hosted resource and the library's discovery and delivery software?
  - Are changes in title coverage communicated in a timely and effective manner?
  - Does library staff receive excellent customer service from content provider representatives?
- License and pricing
  - Is the resource licensed through a third party such as a consortium?
  - Are there any unusual provisions in the license for this resource?
  - What is the cancellation policy for the resource?
  - What is the pricing model and annual subscription price for this resource?
  - Is the price of this resource based on its inclusion in a lager package of resources?
  - If this is a multiyear contract, what is the annual percent increase in the price?
- Usage
  - In what ways were the titles used (e.g., viewed, downloaded) and how often?
  - Are there titles that were used significantly more often than others?
  - What is the average cost per downloaded resource?
  - If the resource is a demand-driven plan
    - How many short-term loans were activated?
    - How many permanent purchases were activated?
    - How many unpurchased titles remain?
    - Are there any noticeable commonalities in the used resources?
    - Are there any trends in the discovery or use of activated resources?p

This baseline information will be augmented in each review cycle with data from the previous year. The recognition of changing conditions requires that the electronic resource librarian is aware of existing conditions as reported in the previous cycle, understands how to collect meaningful, comparable current data, and continually scans the environment for changes in the information landscape.

Much of the data needed to update previous data sets will already be collected and stored by the library. The license and pricing information will be in the library's ERMS, as will basic information about the resource and the content provider. Information about titles and holdings will be available through the knowledge base. Some data, however, will be collected through other means. For instance, it is common to employ a database to record interactions that take place between library staff and vendor representatives. Likewise, the electronic resource librarian often has an in-house knowledge base to record access issues and troubleshooting efforts. This provides a permanent record of not only problems, but also solutions. In this way, the database can be reused by the electronic resource librarian and others as a tool for future troubleshooting.

The electronic resource librarian also relies on external resources to round out the information needed for effective reporting. The environmental scanning that the electronic resource librarian engages in everyday will inform them about new resources, title changes, vendor acquisitions and mergers, and standards development in the area of resource assessment. The electronic resource librarian will also engage often with other library staff on committees in which electronic resources are central. These are opportunities to keep current with the changing needs of the user community, as well as user satisfaction with various resources and platforms. The community profile mentioned earlier will likely be maintained by a collection development librarian or subject liaison.

For a more formal evaluation of user community needs, the electronic resource librarian along with the collection development librarian or subject specialist might elect to administer a survey or host a focus group to ensure that their needs and wants are being addressed.

Other useful external resources that may help inform decision makers about the value of a resource are the proprietary measures of scholarly influence. These measures include Thomson's Impact Factor, the Eigenfactor developed by the University of Washington, and the various journal metrics offered by Elsevier, such as Source-Normalized Impact per Paper, The Impact per Publication, and SCImago Journal Rank. Additionally, there may be new ways to assess scholarly output on the horizon. In June 2013, the Alfred P. Sloan Foundation awarded the National

Information Standards Organization (NISO) a grant to develop new assessment metrics that may diminish the importance often given to the traditional impact factors. Some metrics under consideration by the committee are usage-based metrics, social media references, and network behavioral analysis. The committee is also exploring assessment criteria for nontraditional research outputs, such as data sets, visualizations, software, and other applications (NISO 2015).

USE STATISTICS

An important component of developing meaningful assessment reports is determining the value that the resource provides the library in relation to the money that the library expends to deliver it. Value comprises more than just cost per download, as is evidenced by the list of components that need to be investigated when undergoing the assessment process, but it is a compelling component. Often, administrators want to see the bottom line. Use statistics not only provide a measure that is desired by decision makers, but also are a convenient way to compare the value of resources. In order for these measures to be comparable across resources, data must be collected and treated consistently. This is not as easy as it may seem. More than a decade of standards development has been dedicated to this endeavor.

A suite of protocols and standards has grown around the desire to measure value through the use of electronic resources, both in isolation and in comparison with other resources. In the early days of widespread electronic resources in libraries, there was no consensus by librarians, vendors, and publishers about best to monitor the use of a given resource. Initially, content providers would supply data to electronic resource librarians when requested through a. dat or Excel file delivered via email. A librarian may ask for total number of searches conducted or total number of full-text downloads during a certain time period. The same request to multiple content providers would result in very different statistics. One content provider may provide number of searches based on how many times a user returned to a result screen because the page would be refreshed and recorded as a new search. Another content provider may provide full-text download numbers based on whether the article was downloaded to the webserver to be displayed on the screen, rather than downloaded to an external drive by an end user. Further complicating matters, some content providers would provide data parsed out by month, while others would provide only quarterly data. Some content providers didn't feel that providing use data to libraries was something they needed to worry about.

Since there was no consistency in any aspect of usage data provision, it was up to the electronic resource librarian and the larger community of practice that was growing up around ERM to figure out ways to standardize and streamline data collection and analysis. In 2002, Project COUNTER or Counting Online Usage of Networked Statistics set out to "set standards that facilitate the recording and reporting of online usage statistics in a consistent, credible and compatible way." The first COUNTER Code of Practice, covering online journals and databases, was published in 2003. COUNTER's coverage was extended with the Code of Practice for online books and reference works in 2006. These endeavors have been a boon not only for librarians seeking to compare usage statistics from different content providers, derive useful metrics such as cost per use, make better-informed purchasing decisions, plan infrastructure more effectively, but also for content providers who can satisfy the needs of their library customer base, as well as inform themselves about genuine use patterns.

The COUNTER Code of Practice is a comprehensive document that contains sections defining terms, explanations for and examples of compliant reports (see Table 8.1), requirements for automated harvesting of data, and instructions for implementation and compliance verification. The Project COUNTER website lists all content providers that provide compliant statistics. These content providers have implemented the specified guidelines and have submitted a signed declaration of compliance. There may be a few products that the librarian wishes to license that do not consider libraries to be their primary market and therefore will not feel the investment to become counter compliant worthwhile. They should, however, be able to provide some type of use data. Also, you may use data from website and proxy server logs to get some idea about the community's interest in the resource.

The data were standardized, but it was still up to the electronic resource librarian to gather, compile, and analyze the data manually. This is a time-consuming task that requires visiting each content provider's administrative interface at intervals throughout the year to download data. Efforts were made by NISO and Project COUNTER to standardize the harvesting of these data through automated web services with its protocol called Standardized Usage Harvesting Initiative (SUSHI), ANSI/NISO Z39.93–2014 (NISO 2014a).

Table 8.1 List of COUNTER Usage Reports

Report	Description
Journal Report 1	Number of Successful Full-Text Article Requests by Month and Journal
Journal Report 1 GOA	Number of Successful Gold Open Access Full-Text Article Requests by Month and Journal
Journal Report 1a	Number of Successful Full-Text Article Requests from an Archive by Month and Journal
Journal Report 2	Access Denied to Full-Text Articles by Month, Journal, and Category
Journal Report 3	Number of Successful Item Requests by Month, Journal, and Page-Type
Journal Report 3 Mobile	Number of Successful Item Requests by Month, Journal, and Page-Type for Usage on a Mobile Device
Journal Report 4	Total Searches Run by Month and Collection
Journal Report 5	Number of Successful Full-Text Article Requests by Year-of-Publication (YOP) and Journal
Database Report 1	Total Searches, Result Clicks, and Record Views by Month and Database
Database Report 2	Access Denied by Month, Database, and Category
Platform Report 1	Total Searches, Result Clicks, and Record Views by Month and Platform
Book Report 1	Number of Successful Title Requests by Month and Title
Book Report 2	Number of Successful Section Requests by Month and Title
Book Report 3	Access Denied to Content Items by Month, Title, and Category
Book Report 4	Access Denied to Content items by Month, Platform, and Category

Report	Description
Book Report 5	Total Searches by Month and Title
Multimedia Report 1	Number of Successful Full Multimedia Content Unit Requests by Month and Collection
Multimedia Report 2	Number of Successful Full Multimedia Content Unit Requests by Month, Collection, and Item Type
Title Report 1	Number of Successful Requests for Journal Full-Text Articles and Book Sections by Month and Title
Title Report 1 Mobile	Number of Successful Requests for Journal Full-Text Articles and Book Sections by Month and Title (formatted for normal browsers/delivered to mobile devices AND formatted for mobile devices/delivered to mobile devices
Title Report 2	Access Denied to Full-Text Items by Month, Title, and Category
Title Report 3	Number of Successful Item Requests by Month, Title, and Page Type
Title Report 3 Mobile	Number of Successful Item Requests by Month, Title, and Page Type (formatted for normal browsers/delivered to mobile devices AND formatted for mobile devices/delivered to mobile devices

Source: COUNTER (Counting Online Usage of Networked Electronic Resources). *The COUNTER Code of Practice for e-Resources: Release 4.* April 2012. Retrieved from http://www.projectcounter.org/r4/COPR4.pdf. Used with permission.

This initiative would potentially save the electronic resource librarian valuable time as it was meant to facilitate the automated harvesting and consolidation of usage statistics from different content providers. To aid content providers in complying with these standards, in 2014, NISO has released NISO RP-14–2014 NISO SUSHI Protocol: COUNTER-SUSHI Implementation Profile. It defines a practical implementation structure to be used in the creation of reports and services related to harvesting COUNTER reports using the NISO SUSHI Protocol (NISO 2014b).

These implementation protocols are likely best left to systems personnel if librarians wish to harvest the data with a homegrown system. A company called Scholarly Stats made an early attempt to perform these functions on behalf of libraries. The company was acquired by Swets in 2007, but ceased to exist when Swets was declared bankrupt in 2014. Fortunately, service providers are beginning to include use data harvesting and reporting functionality in their software suites, such as ProQuest's 360 Counter and EBSCONET Usage Consolidation. An open-source ERMS called CORAL has a use reporting module that seems to be meeting with a fair degree of success. Successful harvesting by any of these means, however, is determined by the quality of the data that are being harvested and their associated mapping rules. Providing COUNTER-compliant data is just one piece of the puzzle.

Many electronic resource librarians continue to collect data manually because it takes less time than harvesting the data and then cleaning it up so that it is suitable for analysis. If not using a third-party statistical analysis tool, the final step in creating meaningful reports is to integrate the data with library-specific information such as subscription price. With this combination of data, measures such as of cost per use can be easily generated using basic spreadsheet software. Data sets for different products and/or content providers may also be integrated in order to compare the relative value of one resource to another.

ASSESSMENT REPORTING

The assessment process requires the input from multiple stakeholders. Representatives from the user community, such as students and faculty, may require an analysis based on performance indicators that are quite different from the performance indicators included in a report to the library director. An ongoing formal committee may be an integral component of the assessment process from its initiation. They will have already indicated the type of analysis that will be most useful for their decision-making process. They will review the electronic resource librarian's report and either agree with the recommendations, request further information, or disagree with the analysis and request a revision. Dissenting members of the committee might elect to write alternative recommendations to those provided by the electronic resource librarian for the record.

Decision makers are typically very busy people and count on the electronic resource librarian to synthesize and succinctly communicate the important information required to make sound decisions. The electronic resource librarian should know what decisions will be made using the analysis that is being conducted to ensure optimum relevance. The decision makers likely will have already communicated to the electronic resource librarian which performance indicators they consider to be most important. Reports should always begin with an executive summary highlighting key points, significant changes, and recommendations, in the event that this is all that gets read. The body of the report should illustrate findings and elaborate on the reasoning behind the recommendations. Evidence to substantiate assertions and arguments should be included in appendices. Be direct, clear, and concise.

DESELECTING ELECTRONIC RESOURCES

Occasionally, after careful assessment and review of the electronic resource librarian's reports, the library will elect to cancel a subscription. Many things are considered at this point:

- A careful review of the license and any additional contracts made with the content provider for the resource should be reviewed.
- Ensure that this cancellation will not impact the terms of a contract for any other resource.
- Determine that the library can comply with the cancellation terms set out in the license.
- Notify the content provider of the library's decision.
- Inform your consortium if they brokered the initial license terms.
- Next notify other stakeholders, particularly users of the resource, that it will no longer be available after a certain date and provide an agreed-upon statement for the cancellation.
- Offer suggestions for alternative resources, if they exist.

While electronic resource librarians are under no obligation to discuss why they have made this decision with the content providers, as a professional courtesy, they should be ready to reveal some of the more significant reasons. Further, invested stakeholders should have already been apprised of the assessment under way, and this decision should not come as a surprise (Emery and Stone, 2013b).

There will be a series of technical considerations as well. Just as electronic resource librarians need to set into motion a series of events when implementing a resource for the first time, he or she also needs to take these events out of motion when the resource is being cancelled. Not doing so in a thorough and deliberate manner can lead to frustrated users trying to access a resource that the library no longer subscribes to. Ensure that there is a notice of nonrenewal at all public and internal access points including the A–Z list, catalog record, and knowledge base. As the end of the existing contract nears, ensure that all of the public access points to the resource are cut off. Change the holdings or switch off the resource in the knowledge base. Deactivate the catalog record. Ensure the subject liaisons revise libguides and other materials used for reference and instruction (Emery and Stone 2013b).

ACTIVITY

1. An academic library receives use data for a database that indicates a substantial increase in searches performed and articles downloaded over the previous reporting period. What other data might you gather to explain the dramatic increase? Why would that data be useful?

REFERENCES

Emery, J and G. Stone. 2013a. "Annual Review." In *Techniques for Electronic Resource Management. Library Technology Reports*, February/March 2013. Chicago: American Library Association.

Emery, J and G. Stone. 2013b. "Cancellation and Replacement Review." In *Techniques for Electronic Resource Management. Library Technology Reports*, February/March 2013. Chicago: American Library Association.

National Information Standards Organization. 2014a. "Standardized Usage Statistics Harvesting Initiative (SUSHI) Protocol (ANSI/NISO Z39.93–2014)." Baltimore: National Information Standards Organization. Retrieved from http://www.niso.org/workrooms/sushi.

National Information Standards Organization. 2014b. "NISO RP-14–2014 NISO SUSHI Protocol: COUNTER-SUSHI Implementation Profile." Baltimore: National Information Standards Organization. Retrieved from http://www.niso.org/apps/group_public/project/details.php?project_id=123.

National Information Standards Organization. 2015. "NISO Alternative Assessment Metrics (Altmetrics) Initiative." Baltimore: National Information Standards Organization. Retrieved from http://www.niso.org/topics/tl/altmetrics_initiative/.

ProjectCOUNTER. 2015. "Codes of practice." ProjectCOUNTER. Retrieved from http://www.projectcounter.org/code_practice.html.

Chapter 9
Preserving Electronic Resources

The topic of preserving electronic resources has the potential to quickly become unmanageably large if electronic resources are considered in the very broadest sense as anything created in digital format. Indeed, there are efforts in progress to do that, to preserve the World Wide Web. The International Internet Preservation Organization (http://www.netpreserve.org), the Internet Archive's Wayback Machine (https://archive.org/web/), and the Library of Congress's Twitter Archive are just a few examples.

However, in order to answer some of the questions asked in this chapter, it is necessary to narrow down the scope of what is being preserved. Authors, publishers, libraries, institutions of higher education and other institutions of which libraries are a part, agencies funding the research reported in electronic formats, and collaborative groups of the former all have a stake in preserving their electronic content just as they have in preserving content in other formats. Thus, in this chapter, the focus will be the preservation of the types of electronic resources that have been discussed thus far in the book: electronic resources that are collected, organized, promoted, vetted by virtue of being included in a library collection, subscribed, and licensed by and in libraries. Some important issues that arise for those committed to preserving electronic resources such as where responsibility for preserving electronic resources lies, sustainability, selecting what to preserve, perpetual access, and the role of public policy in preservation activities are discussed. The chapter concludes with some examples of current initiatives aimed at preserving electronic resources in order to highlight the variety of approaches to preserving electronic resources.

PRESERVATION ISSUES
Whose Responsibility Is It?

As there is with preserving all manner of materials, there is no one clear answer to the question who is responsible for preserving electronic resources. Over the past two decades, as electronic journals and electronic books proliferated at an exponential rate, the question has been raised by any number of entities and answered in many different ways. Academic libraries have traditionally been viewed primarily for storing the record of scholarship and research in the form of print journals. Preservation of print journals included binding journal volumes into hardcover and recording them on microforms. Now, however, not only has the amount of scholarly content greatly expanded, but also both the forms in which it is communicated and the forums in which it is being expressed have expanded. No longer are the scholarly journal article and the scholarly monograph the sole sources of recorded scholarship. Scholars are sharing research results in social media. Those funding research are asking that not only research results but also research data be published.

Several very successful electronic resources preservation initiatives currently exist. Supported by for-profit and not-for-profit entities, created and managed by librarians, library consortia, publishers, scholars, and civic-minded entrepreneurs, these initiatives have very different missions related to preserving scholarship and very different approaches to accomplishing it. Besides the fact that a great deal of electronic content is not being preserved, one challenge related to these initiatives is that they don't cover the same content; what they do cover in common is not covered in the same way (*Preservation Status of E-Resources* 2011). As an example, Portico ingests scholarly content and converts it to a standardized look and feel so that items retrieved from Portico contain the original scholarly content but not, for example, the publisher's marketing materials. On the other hand, Lots Of Copies Keep Stuff Safe (LOCKSS) ingests and preserves the scholarly content of electronic journals exactly as it appeared in the original publication.

Authors, publishers, libraries, institutions of higher education and other institutions of which libraries are a part, agencies funding the research reported in electronic formats, and collaborative groups of the former all have a stake in preserving their content just as they have in preserving content in other formats. Given the amount of scholarly content now being published, it will take concerted effort and collaboration among all these stakeholders to preserve the scholarly and cultural record for future generations.

Sustainability

Similar to nonprint physical formats for communicating information, the sustainability of electronic information formats presents a particular challenge in terms of sustaining access to their content: obsolescence of the device required to extract and make the information content human readable. A book requires no mediation in order for its contents to be human readable; simply pick it up and open it. A microform, a sound recording on a cassette tape, a film on DVD, a journal article or electronic book in ePub format, and a Twitter conversation about the results of a recent experiment all require mediation of a device and/or technology in order for a human to make sense of their content.

From a preservation perspective, not only must the information container itself be preserved, the device and/or technology required to access its content must also be preserved. Clearly, this requirement adds to the complexity and cost of preserving electronic and other types of resources. Newer versions of word processing software provide a good example. Many versions of Microsoft Word are backward compatible to some extent, but there is far less chance that the content of an electronic document created using WordPerfect in 1982 will be accessible to an average user in 2020. For this reason, some preservation initiatives, notably Portico, have elected not only to convert the content in their archives to a file format that is currently accessible but also to continue to migrate that content to new file formats as necessary to preserve access.

Backward compatibility means that newer versions of a piece of software are capable of interaction with, that is opening, manipulating, and so on, depending on the purpose of the software, artifacts created using older versions of the software. New versions of software lacking backward compatibility would render artifacts created with older versions inaccessible via the new versions. Providing backward compatibility of newer versions is particularly important for proprietary software for which a consumer has paid a large sum. It is usually provided for one or two earlier versions of a piece of software but not all of them, especially when there have been multiple versions. At some point, the software publisher requires customers to purchase a newer version of the software.

What to Preserve

One of the challenges of preserving electronic resources, even limiting it to the record of scholarship in electronic format, is the proliferation of formats and forums in which it is published. Traditional channels for communicating scholarship in electronic journals have existed far longer than some of the new channels like social media. Thus, it is easy to understand why systems for preserving content communicated via these channels are further along in development than are those devoted to preserving new communications channels. For example, the Library of Congress initiated a project to preserve the content of Twitter in 2010. However, as of 2013, they are still "confronting and working around the technology challenges to making the archive accessible to researchers and policymakers in a comprehensive, useful way" (Library of Congress 2013, 1).

Most efforts to preserve the content of electronic resources have been focused on research and scholarship. Most of the preservation initiatives covered in the next section were launched by research libraries, scholarly publishers, and nonprofit agencies devoted to preserving the scholarly record. But what about works of fiction? Public libraries are embracing electronic books, both electronic texts and streaming audiobooks, because their customers are demanding them. Less effort has been made to preserve electronic fiction. Initiatives like Project Gutenberg and the Google Books project are making efforts to preserve and distribute classic fiction that is in the public domain. Far less effort has been made to preserve newer forms of fiction such as self-published books or fan fiction.

Fan fiction is the popular name for a recent development in fiction writing, the use of another author's fictional characters, settings, and so on, in a new story or work, usually by fans of the original work. It is most often self-published and freely available on the Internet. It has created a large variety of new copyright issues that are beyond the scope of this chapter. A good starting point for learning more about these issues is Lipton's (2014) article "Copyright and the Commercialization of Fan Fiction."

Perpetual Access

Perpetual access is so strongly assumed for physical formats of information containers that it is rarely discussed. Unless the equipment required to access their contents becomes obsolete, once a library has purchased a physical information container like a book, a journal, or a DVD, the library owns it and may do with it, within the confines of copyright laws, what it pleases in perpetuity. The same cannot be said for many subscribed electronic resources. Subscribed electronic resources in libraries are much more often licensed than purchased outright simply because the cost of purchasing them, either individually or as a collection, is far too high for most libraries to afford. In addition, the content providers from whom these resources are licensed often provide a great deal of added value to electronic resource in the form of indexing, abstracts, search interfaces, faceted results, free storage space in which users may create personalized collections, and the ability for libraries to customize a resource's appearance. Librarians should carefully examine the licenses and contracts in which their rights for accessing the resource content are set out. They will need to negotiate specifically for the right to have perpetual access to the resource content to which they are subscribing. Otherwise, unlike a subscription to a print journal, when the subscription is cancelled, the library and its customers lose access to the content of the resource.

Like sustainability discussed earlier, perpetual access or the lack thereof creates complexities for preserving electronic resource that do not exist for physical resources. Publishers and librarians alike must devise means for library customers to have continual access to such content even in the event that a publisher ceases operation, a publisher stops publishing a title, a publisher no longer offers back issues, or "catastrophic and sustained failure of a publisher's delivery platform" (Portico 2015b). Portico and LOCKSS are examples of initiatives that address the issue of perpetual

writing and scholarship on a personal computer or as formal as the large preservation initiatives covered in the rest of this section. They may be fee based with stringent policies and procedures for deposit, storage, retrieval, access, and so on, or freely accept any and every item offered to them.

Institutional repositories have become popular in institutions of higher education in recent years partly due to the growing availability and affordability of software developed for the sole purpose of repository management. Other factors influencing their growing popularity include the availability of open-source repository software, the increasing public policy-driven move toward open access, and technological advances that have dramatically lowered the cost of storage. Institutional repositories exist at individual institutions, and consortial, state, and national levels. For illustrative purposes, repositories at the level of the individual institution will be considered here with the understanding that most of the characteristics discussed translate to larger repositories.

An institutional repository serves as a collection and, usually, open-access distribution point for digital materials produced by entities associated with the institution. They often include the written work of scholars, both faculty and students, of the institution that has been published elsewhere like journal articles, and other types of materials like audio and video and the data upon which the scholarship is based. Creating and maintaining an institutional repository often falls to the institution's library although recently larger institutions especially are creating specialized positions and departments for this purpose. An institutional repository serves additional purposes within an institution including providing a means for the institution to communicate the benefits the institution provides to its surrounding community, a means of complying with a growing number of tax-supported funding agencies' mandates that the results of funded research be made freely available to tax payers, as well as a method for preserving the institution's contributions to scholarship.

How It Works

Creating an institutional repository usually begins with the development and/or implementation of repository software, which generally includes a metadata schema for describing the items ingested into it and user interfaces for search and retrieval as well as deposit. Many choices are available to choose from including fee-based (e.g., ContentDM) and open-source (e.g., DSpace) repository software packages. Basic repository functionality includes a means for ingesting, uploading, content files to a designated storage space, which may be hosted locally or remotely. Open-source repository software is generally locally hosted; that is, the content is stored on a server local to the institution. A remotely hosted repository is generally fee based since, although much less costly than it was two decades ago, storage space usually comes at a cost. It also includes a means for ingesting and/or creating metadata associated with content for search and retrieval purposes as well as for preservation purposes and to describe ownership and other rights associated with the ingested content. Finally, repository software usually includes a user interface through which individuals and computers can search for and retrieve, at the very least, information about the repository's content. The complexity of repository software and the technical expertise to use it generally increase with the size of the repository.

Google Books

Google works with libraries, publishers, and authors "to create a comprehensive, searchable, virtual card catalog of all books in all languages that helps users discover new books and publishers discover new readers" (Google Books 2015) and provides varying levels of full-text content to the public via its Google Books platform. This massive project includes partnerships with publishers, libraries, and individual authors. In the Partner Program, Google works with publishers to include bibliographic information about the publisher's books in the Google database. The publisher may also choose to allow Google to display varying amounts of a book's content, up to the entire text, or to display no text at all but merely provide a link to sources where users may find the full text of the book such as in their local library, a bookstore, or online purchase. The Partner Program also includes individual authors. The Library Project is a partnership between Google and large libraries worldwide to digitize and catalog the contents of their collection. Such libraries as the Austrian National Library, the New York Public Library, and the Oxford University Library are participants in the Google Library Program. In cases where the materials owned by these libraries are still under copyright, Google displays to users only a few sentences from the full text called a "snippet." The work that Google is doing has created controversy and even legal action, the description of which is beyond the scope of this chapter. Band (2006) is a good starting point for further information.

How It Works

Although some of Google's agreements with libraries in its Library Project are public, many are not, leaving the specifics of how Google works with these entities unclear. This practice is part of the basis for the controversy mentioned earlier. In general, Google's Library Project partner libraries supply printed books from their collections to Google. Google scans the books using a book scanning process it created and patented that allows scanning of up to 1,000 pages per hour. The books are then returned to the library that owns them, and Google makes the digitized content accessible to the public on its Google Books platform. How much of the book's content is made available is determined by several factors including whether the book is under copyright and Google's agreement with the library that owns it. At a minimum, Google provides bibliographic information about a book along with information about where the full contents of the book can be obtained. In the intermediate range, with the permission of the copyright owner, Google may provide access to anywhere from a few pages of content up to the entire contents of a book on its Google Books platform. The full content of books in the public domain can be accessed on the Google Books platform. A major advantage of the Google Books platform is that, whether or not the full contents of the book are freely available on the Google Books platform, they are searchable.

HathiTrust

The HathiTrust is a cooperative library of digitized-from-print materials, both in copyright and in the public domain, which exist in member libraries. Its primary constituents are the students, faculty, and staff of member libraries, but, secondarily, it makes materials available to the public within the bounds of copyright and license agreements. Its mission is based in the notion of the common good: "to contribute to research, scholarship, and the common good by collaboratively collecting, organizing, preserving, communicating, and sharing the record of human knowledge" (HathiTrust Digital Library 2015c). It is governed by board of directors who are elected by the membership from among the member institutions. As of this writing, it has a set of short-term objectives and a set of long-term objectives. Short-term objectives center around (1) improving ease of use both for those seeking to use the materials it contains such as the development of a page turner mechanism and access mechanisms for persons with disabilities and (2) identifying standards for member institutions wishing to contribute materials to the collection. Long-term objectives focus on developing underlying technology to improve access and discovery and the integration of more types of materials such as data sets. HathiTrust collections include "digitized book and journal content from the partner libraries. . .[such as] materials digitized by Google, the Internet Archive, and Microsoft, as well as through in-house initiatives" (HathiTrust Digital Library 2015d).

How It Works

HathiTrust targets for membership research libraries and consortia with large amounts of digital content and strong digitization programs. Membership fees are devoted not only to its preservation efforts but also to the development of new services and functionality. Membership fees are paid annually and are calculated using a formula that takes into account the numbers of both in-copyright and public domain titles that are, or will be upon ingestion, unique to HathiTrust; the number institutional members holding in-copyright items; the number of institutional members; and infrastructure costs.

Member libraries may contribute content via removable media or server upload as well as by providing authorization for inclusion of content from the Google Books project and the Internet Archive. Acceptable file formats are TIFF ITU G4, JP2, and Unicode OCR. Content files are accompanied by extensive metadata including bibliographic metadata, preservation metadata (using METS), and rights metadata. The library depositing the content is responsible for reviewing the quality of the content according to HathiTrust's quality guidelines. They are also responsible for providing rights information and permissions for use of the submitted content although HathiTrust staff also conduct manual copyright review of materials published between 1923 and 1963. Once ingested, content is indexed and stored. Deposit of Google content and Internet Archive content involves the member institution giving Google permission to release digital content files to the HathiTrust. All member libraries and their customers may create collections within the HathiTrust interface (HathiTrust Digital Library 2015a; HathiTrust Digital Library 2015b).

Removable media refers to media upon which content is recorded and which is then removed from the computer where the recording was done, physically transferred, for example, by mail, to Hathi, inserted into a computer that can read it. Flash drives and CD-ROMS are examples of removable media. Server upload refers to the transfer of files electronically from one computer to another, for example, by File Transfer Protocol, FTP.

LOCKSS

Lots Of Copies Keep Stuff Safe, or LOCKSS, is a program operated by Stanford University Libraries comprising networks of libraries and publishers operating open-source software for electronic content preservation. The underlying principle of decentralized, distributed preservation is that maintaining copies of digital content in multiple archives provides assurance that the last copy is much less likely to disappear. Another underlying principle is the idea that libraries own the content they pay for, even when that content is subscribed, and they should therefore be allowed to preserve that content. LOCKSS characterizes this as "restoring the print purchase model with which librarians are familiar. . . analogous to libraries' using their own buildings, shelves and staff to obtain, preserve and provide access to paper content . . . restoring libraries' ability to build and preserve local collections" (LOCKSS 2015c). Participating libraries are members of LOCKSS networks who share and compare archived content in order to ensure its accuracy and integrity.

How It Works

LOCKSS member publishers give permission for LOCKSS member libraries to preserve subscribed content. LOCKSS libraries use the LOCKSS software to create a local, online "LOCKSS box" with web access in order to communicate with content providers and a LOCKSS network with which the library has registered. The LOCKSS box ingests library-subscribed content from publisher member websites using a web crawler, continually compares the ingested content with that contained in other LOCKSS boxes in the LOCCKS network to which the library belongs, delivers content to library customers when necessary, provides the library with the ability to manage the content of its LOCKSS box, and migrates preserved content to new formats as necessary (LOCKSS 2015a). Ingesting new content is facilitated by the use of a static IP address (within the library's network IP range), which the content publisher uses to identify authorized LOCKSS libraries and the content to which they are subscribed. Content is ingested exactly as it appears on the publisher's site so that "the 'look and feel' of the content, along with the publishers' branding, is preserved, resulting in an authentic representation of the authoritative source file" (LOCKSS 2015b). Delivery of LOCKSS content occurs when the stored content becomes unavailable from the publisher's website (including after the library's subscription is cancelled). The LOCKSS box acts as a proxy server and an OpenURL server to provide content to library customers. Managing the content of a LOCKSS box is achieved using a web interface and consists of selecting new content to be ingested and generating reports on the locally preserved content. Membership in LOCKSS is free to publishers. Member libraries make a financial contribution to LOCKSS based on their size. U.S. libraries are measured on a scale loosely based on Carnegie classification.

Portico

Like LOCKSS, Portico is a dark archive, that is, a repository for digital materials, whose primary purpose is preservation and whose materials are inaccessible. In Portico's case, the archive remains dark until a trigger event occurs, such as when a publisher ceases operation, a publisher stops publishing a title, a publisher no longer offers back issues, "catastrophic and sustained failure of a publisher's delivery platform" (Portico 2015b). It is part of Ithaka, a "not-for-profit organization that helps the academic community use digital technologies to preserve the scholarly record and to advance research and teaching in sustainable ways" (Ithaka 2015), along with JSTOR, the database and Ithaka S+R, the research arm of Ithaka.

How It Works

Portico has two primary sets of customers, libraries and publishers, to whom it offers a suite of complimentary services in exchange for content and financial contributions. Publishers make an annual financial contribution to Portico for these services, and this varies based on the publisher's annual journal and/or eBook revenues. Publishers deposit e-journal and eBook content with Portico via portable media (e.g., CDs, magnetic tape), FTP (File Transfer Protocol), or OAI-PMH (the Open Archives Initiative - Protocol for Metadata Harvesting, a tool for collecting metadata). In return, Portico processes the content it receives from publishers according to its preservation plan and then monitors the content in order to keep it both secure and accessible. Libraries are charged an annual financial contribution to Portico with an amount based on the amount spent on materials purchases annually. In return, upon the occurrence of a trigger event, Portico provides the library with access to the archival copies held in Portico's archive to which the library subscribed prior to the trigger event. Access is usually provided via a web-based platform similar to an electronic resources database and according to conditions set out in a license agreement between the library and Portico.

FTP is "the TCP/IP protocol that allows data files to be copied directly from one computer to another over the Internet regardless of platform, without having to attach them as in e-mail" (Reitz 2015).

The Portico archive contains the content submitted by publishers, which it has repackaged in archival file formats specialized for preservation. These file formats allow Portico to provide both HTML and PDF versions of publisher content in a standardized way. They exclude the publisher's original e-commerce customization and the library's original customization of the publisher's or aggregator's platform. Portico allows a small number of individuals from member libraries and member publishers to have access to the dark archive in order to "engage in an independent verification of the Portico archive's integrity" (Portico 2015a).

Other Preservation Initiatives of Note

Many other preservation initiatives exist around the world. This list contains some of the most noteworthy of them.

- E-Depot is a Netherlands-based project for preserving the content of journals in the Directory of Open Access Journals (DOAJ).
- ArXiv (http://arxiv.org) is a collection of scholarly article preprints in the disciplines of physics, mathematics, computer science, qualitative biology,

quantitative finance, and statistics owned and operated by Cornell University containing over 1 million papers.

- CLOCKSS, which stands for Controlled Lots Of Copies Keep Stuff Safe, is an instantiation of LOCKSS and therefore works very similarly to LOCKSS although content and policy differs from LOCKSS.
- 2CUL is a partnership between Columbia University Libraries and Cornell University Libraries part of which involves e-journal preservation.

ACTIVITY

1. Choose a library with which you are familiar or one with which to become familiar. Which of the preservation initiatives described in this chapter (or combination of initiatives) would best suit this library's desire to preserve its digital content?

REFERENCES

Association of Research Libraries. 2002. "Removal or Destruction of Federal Depository Library Documents." Association of Research Libraries. Retrieved from http://www.arl.org/storage/documents/publications/susman_fdlp_march02.pdf.

Band, Jonathan. 2006. "The Google Library Project: Both Sides of the Story." *Plagiary: Cross-Disciplinary Studies in Plagiarism, Fabrication, and Falsification.* Retrieved from http://hdl.handle.net/2027/spo.5240451.0001.002.

Google Books. 2015. "Google Books Library Project." Google Books. Accessed June 15. Retrieved from https://www.google.com/googlebooks/library/.

Hakala, Juha. 2001. "Libraries, Metadata and Preservation of Electronic Resources." Proceedings of the IATUL Conference 2001. Retrieved from http://docs.lib .purdue.edu/cgi/viewcontent.cgi?article=1545&context=iatul.

HathiTrust Digital Library. 2015a. "Guidelines for Digital Object Deposit." Accessed June 15. Retrieved from http://www.hathitrust.org/deposit_guidelines.

HathiTrust Digital Library. 2015b. "Ingest Checklist." Accessed June 15. Retrieved from http://www.hathitrust.org/ingest_checklist.

HathiTrust Digital Library. 2015c. "Mission and Goals." HathiTrust. Accessed June 15. Retrieved from http://www.hathitrust.org/mission_goals.

HathiTrust Digital Library. 2015d. "Our Partnership." HathiTrust. Accessed June 15. Retrieved from http://www.hathitrust.org/partnership.

Ithaka. 2015. "Our Mission." Ithaca. Retrieved from http://ithaka.org/mission-old.

Library of Congress. 2013. "Update on the Twitter Archive at the Library of Congress." Library of Congress. h Retrieved from ttp://www.loc.gov/today/pr/2013/files/twitter_report_2013jan.pdf.

Lipton, Jacqueline D. 2014. "Copyright and the Commercialization of Fanfiction." *Houston Law Review* 52 (2): 425–66.

LOCKSS. 2015a. "How LOCKSS Works." LOCKSS. Accessed June 14. Retrieved from http://www.lockss.org/about/how-it-works/.

LOCKSS. 2015b. "Preservation Principles." LOCKSS. Accessed June 14. Retrieved from http://www.lockss.org/about/principles/.

LOCKSS. 2015c. "What Is LOCKSS?" LOCKSS. Accessed June 14. Retrieved from http://www.lockss.org/about/what-is-lockss/.

National Institutes of Health. 2014. "When and How to Comply." National Institutes of Health. Retrieved from https://publicaccess.nih.gov/.

Portico. 2015a. "Archive Content & Access." Portico. Retrieved from http://www.portico.org/digital-preservation/the-archive-content-access.

Portico. 2015b. "Preservation Step-by-Step." Portico. Retrieved from http://www.portico.org/digital-preservation/services/preservation-approach/preservation-step-by-step#step5.

Preservation Status of E-Resources: A Potential Crisis in Electronic Journal Preservation. 2011. Retrieved from http://www.cni.org/topics/digital-preservation/preservation-status-of-eresources/.

Reitz, Joan. 2015. *ODLIS: Online Dictionary of Library and Information Science.* Retrieved from http://lu.com/odlis/search.cfm.

Chapter 10
Scholarly Communication

Scholarly communication refers to the "the creation, transformation, dissemination, and preservation of knowledge related to teaching, research, and scholarly endeavors" (Radom, Feltner-Reichert, and Stringer-Stanback 2012, 106). Although it is not limited to work conducted by scholars and researchers in academic institutions, their work, as opposed to that of researchers in commercial enterprises, makes up the bulk of scholarly communication. The traditional venues for scholarly communication are journal articles, monographs or books, and conference proceedings. The relative proportion of use of each venue varies from one academic discipline to another for reasons that will be explored in more depth in this chapter.

Although the process of scholarly communication is an iterative one, an appropriate and typical starting point for a description of it is the conduct of research and creative activity in the sense of both the conduct of a research protocol and the search for existing knowledge in libraries. Traditionally, scholars and researchers share the results of their research and creative activity in written reports, which "can be descriptions of original research, theory, review of research and or theory or opinion pieces" (Morrison 2009, 15); however, the arts are a notable exception to this because the results of creative activity in many arts disciplines are not textual in nature, for example, music, dance, and visual arts. Written reports of scholarly activity are often vetted in a process called

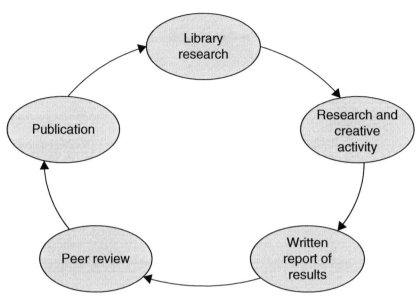

Figure 10.1 The flow of scholarly publishing.

peer review, "a more or less rigorous examination [of a manuscript] by two or more members of the author's peer group, traditionally remaining anonymous" (Swan 2006, 6). Once reviewed, they are published in journals, monographs, and conference proceedings. The journals, monographs, and conference proceedings are collected, organized, made accessible, and preserved in libraries and other information agencies where scholars may find, select, identify, and obtain them, and the process begins again. Figure 10.1 is a simple illustration of the process.

> It has become appropriate to include the creative activities of musicians, artists, and creative writers in definitions of scholarship in the scholarly communication process because in institutions of higher education, faculty in these disciplines are evaluated for tenure and promotion upon their creative output just as faculty in science, social science, and humanities disciplines are evaluated on their scholarly output.

This, of course, is a simplified description of an extremely complex process that has developed and evolved over almost 350 years, one that a myriad of authors have covered in full-length books, one to which multiple organizations are devoted. Clearly, the aspects of scholarly communication that can be covered in a single chapter of this book are severely limited. Thus, the objective of this chapter is to create a basic understanding of the processes and entities that are involved in scholarly publishing, the roles that they play and their relationships with one another, and the things that influence the processes of scholarly communication in the context of managing electronic resources as defined in earlier chapters.

MAJOR PLAYERS IN SCHOLARLY COMMUNICATION

Scholars and researchers, publishers, librarians, and funding agencies all play major roles in the process of scholarly communication. The easiest way to describe their roles in the process is to discuss them individually, but this can create a false sense of separation among them. In reality, they are inextricably interwoven, often taking one role at one stage of the process and another role at another stage. For instance, librarians' role in the process of scholarly communication is to collect, organize, make accessible, and preserve the products of scholarly endeavors. But librarians are also scholars, conductors of research, and creators of new knowledge. Librarians may also take the role of publisher as they manage institutional repositories in which manuscripts and other information resources that are the result of scholarly and creative activity are deposited. Thus, the reader is encouraged to think of the major players described here as roles of which a single individual may play more than one.

Defining Research

The term "research" in the context of the process of scholarly communication can have two very different meanings. It can mean the design, conduct, evaluation, and reporting on the results of a research study. It can also mean searching the literature of a particular field or fields using electronic resources, other library resources such as printed scholarly journals and monographs, and other sources outside the library such as the web. For the purposes of this discussion, we will call the former "research" and the latter "library research" even though this type of research occurs outside of the library as well as inside it.

Scholars and Researchers

The process of scholarly communication arguably both begins and ends with scholars and researchers. They produce new knowledge and communicate it, as well as use the end products, which are sometimes collectively called research outputs, of others' research and creative activity. Scholars and researchers in higher education are usually not rewarded financially for publishing the results of their research and creative activity. Rather, their reward for producing new knowledge is increasing their, and by association their institution's, reputation and prestige as well as by earning promotion and tenure. Just as workers in other fields may be rewarded for good work by being promoted to positions of greater responsibility and remuneration, scholars and researchers are rewarded for excelling in some combination of research, teaching, and volunteer service by being promoted to positions of greater prestige and responsibility within their institution. We will discuss the specific impact of the promotion and tenure system on the process of scholarly communication in more detail later. Despite the prestige associated with publishing new knowledge via traditional channels, more and more scholars and researchers are turning to new communication channels made possible by advances in communications technology.

Because new research often begins with scholars and researchers conducting library research, there is the expectation among them that their institutional libraries will own or lease the information resources they need. They can exert a great deal of pressure on library collection development and budgets. Scholars compete with each other for funding for their research from entities both internal and external to their institutions including tax-supported government agencies and private agencies. Unfortunately, more often than not, those research funds are not earmarked for the purchase of library or other information resources. Scholars and researchers also play a role in publishing through participation in the peer-review process. In terms of costs and rewards, the peer-review process works by barter. Scholars and researchers are not asked to pay for the time and effort of peers to review their work, but rather they volunteer their service to review, in turn, the work of their peers. The peer-review process is usually blind and often double-blind, meaning that a scholar/researcher author does not know the identity of the scholar/researcher reviewers and the scholar/researcher reviewers do not know the identity of the scholar/researcher author. This, in addition to the lack of payments, helps to maintain the integrity of the peer-review process.

Publishers

The role of the publisher in the process of scholarly communication seems straightforward; it is to manage the process of communicating new knowledge created by scholars and researchers. Publishers of scholarly information run the gamut in size and purpose: from diversified, multinational, for-profit companies like Elsevier, John Wiley & Sons, and Taylor & Francis who publish thousands of journals and monographs, to small, nonprofit scholarly societies who publish a single scholarly journal.

Advances in communications technology and the advent of electronic publishing have been both extremely advantageous for publishers and extremely challenging. For example, those outside the publishing world believe that there is little or no cost to publishing digital content and therefore expect the cost of purchase (or lease) to be low. Publishers, however, are challenged to create and maintain the infrastructure for delivering, organizing, and preserving electronic content, activities that they have not been called upon to do before and therefore were not employing staff or equipment to do. This is not to say that publishers do not embrace the ability to deliver electronic content; they do, many of them with enthusiasm. They continually work with those who play other roles in the process of scholarly communication to improve and enhance their products.

Librarians have great influence with publishers (although some publishers will argue vociferously to the contrary) because they are among the publishers' largest customers. Librarians purchase more information resources than individuals from publishers of scholarly content, and they pay higher prices for those resources. Advances in technology complicated both the delivery of information resources and the pricing models applied to their purchase, and librarians and publishers do not always agree on the results.

The same is true of scholars' and researchers' interactions with one another in the process of scholarly communication. In a world where scholarly communication was accomplished almost entirely in print, it was typical for scholars and researchers to assign all of their copyrights in their manuscripts to the publisher. This meant that an academic library had to purchase the information resource in which the results of research being done at their own institution because there was no other legal means for the scholar to easily and affordably disseminate their manuscripts. The advent of the Internet not only made it possible but also made it easy and affordable for scholars and researchers to share their manuscripts with their colleagues, for example, via email, a personal or institutional website, or social media. But in order to obtain the trustworthiness and authority conveyed through the peer-review process, scholars and researchers had to continue to publish their manuscripts in scholarly journals and assign at least some of their copyrights to the journal publishers.

Funding agencies' influence with publishers has also increased with the move to electronic publishing. The open-access movement, which is covered in more detail later, has resulted in new business models for publishers. In very simple terms, open access means making scholarly and research output freely available on the Internet to anyone who wishes to consume it. However, as has been mentioned, there are still costs associated with publishing electronic content. One of the new business models shifts these costs from the consumer, that is the subscriber or user, to the author. Unlike funding for the purchase of information resources to support a research project, funding for the cost of publishing the results of a research project in a prestigious scholarly journal is now regularly included in research funding.

Funding Agencies

Funding agencies are those organizations that provide financial support for the conduct of research beyond that available from a scholar or researcher's home institution. Scholars and researchers and their institutions obtain almost as much prestige associated with winning a large research grant as they have for being published in a highly ranked scholarly journal. Some funding agencies are public in that the grant funds they distribute are collected from citizens in the form of taxes. Others are private, depending on donations from individuals as well as organizations.

In simple terms, the grant funding process consists of the funding agency deciding what kinds of research and other scholarly projects it wishes to support. Such decisions are often influenced by the original source of the funds. For example, the National Institutes of Health (NIH) typically funds health-related research and the Institute of Library and Museum Services (IMLS) typically funds research related to libraries and museums. The funding agency then makes public the availability of funds and a description of the process by which scholars and researchers may apply for those funds. Typically, there are more applications for funds than there are available funds, so applications are reviewed and ranked, and the funds granted and distributed to those projects with the highest ranking.

Grant funds always have conditions about how they may be used, and at the very least, funding agencies usually require that the grant awardee reports to them the results of the funded research. One condition that has had particular influence on the process of scholarly communication is one that is usually associated with public, government funding. It is the requirement that the results of the research be made freely and publicly available, that is, open access, if not immediately upon their production, then within a short time afterwards.

Libraries

In the context of a book about electronic resources in libraries, there should be little need to explain the basic function of libraries; thus, this discussion will focus on libraries' and librarians' role in the process of scholarly communication. Some have already been mentioned, for instance, librarians' relationships with publisher as a large proportion of publishers' customers and the expectation of scholars and researchers that libraries will purchase or subscribe to those information resources that are needed for the conduct of research. Librarians play additional roles in the process of scholarly communication as agents for preserving the scholarly record and for assisting scholars and researchers to find and use scholarly resources.

The creation and management of institutional repositories has fallen to libraries more often than not over the past two decades. Recall from Chapter 9 that a repository is "The physical space (building, room, area) reserved for the permanent or intermediate storage of archival materials (manuscripts, rare books, government documents, papers, photographs, etc.) (Reitz 2015). In the context of preserving electronic resources, a repository contains a collection of digital files organized for both searching and finding and archival purposes. In addition to serving to fulfill funding agencies' open-access mandates, institutional repositories serve as a record and archive of an institution's research output. It is often difficult for librarians to persuade scholars and researchers of the benefits of depositing their manuscript in an institution repository since doing so adds no prestige to their publications and requires them to make additional effort to secure or retain the copyrights that allow them to do so.

MAJOR INFLUENCES ON SCHOLARLY COMMUNICATION

In the previous section, there was brief mention of several events and entities that have had strong influences on the process of scholarly communication relevant to the management of electronic resources. This section is a deeper exploration of several of them, particularly as relates to the management of electronic resources in libraries and information agencies.

Technology

As has been covered in earlier chapters and so should be clear by this point in the book, technology has had probably the greatest impact on scholarly communication because it has changed the content of what is being communicated, the means by which communication is accomplished, and the behavior of the communicators. Of the myriad software, hardware, devices, and activities to which the term refers, the Internet is likely the thing that has had the most influence. Combined with a dramatic decrease in the cost of storage for digital files, the Internet makes it possible for scholars who are separated by great distances geographically to easily and instantly share data sets, lab notes, audio and video files, all of the output that is generated in the process of the conduct of scholarly and creative activity. Web 2.0 and social networking have increased the ways in which scholars could communicate with one another as well as the amount of communication. Not only are scholars able to share content more quickly and easily, but they are also generating scholarly content in many new forms. Examples of newly created means of communicating scholarly content are abundant. Social networks of scholars, Tweets about conference programs, scholarly blogs, even email have increased the pace of information scholarly communication to lightning speed.

Open Access

Open Access (OA) refers to the free and unrestricted availability of scholarly literature on the public internet, permitting any users to read, download, copy, distribute, print, search, or link to the full texts of these articles, crawl them for indexing, pass them as data to software, or use them for any other lawful purpose, without financial, legal, or technical barriers other than those inseparable from gaining access to the internet itself. The only constraint on reproduction and distribution, and the only role for copyright in this domain, should be to give authors control over the integrity of their work and the right to be properly acknowledged and cited. ("Budapest Open Access Initiative" 2002)

The members of the Budapest Open Access Initiative reasoned that the work of scholars is "given to the world without expectation of payment," and therefore access to it should not be restricted by the requirement that a fee be paid. The advancement of science and thus the public good would be better and more efficiently served if this information were freely and openly available.

It is important to remember that although most open-access journals are published in electronic format, it should not be assumed that open access equals electronic. The concept of open access was conceived a decade or more before the Internet became a viable channel for widespread dissemination of the results of scholarly activity, but it became a viable possibility only as Internet use became ubiquitous. Both types of open access, green OA and gold OA, rely on the Internet. Green OA is characterized by the dissemination of the results of scholarly activity through scholars themselves using their own websites, email, and so on, as well as institutional repositories. It thus requires that authors retain the right to do so in contracts for publication. Gold OA is characterized by the dissemination of the results of scholarly activity in online open-access journals, that is, scholarly journals for which there is no subscription fee. Although the cost of publishing and disseminating a journal online is substantially lower than the cost of publishing and distributing a print journal, there are still costs associated with publication and distribution such as managing peer review, editing, copyediting, and promotion. For that reason, gold OA is accompanied by the requirement that the author pay the publisher a fee. This remains a major point of contention between publishers and OA advocates.

When open-access journals first developed, many scholars considered the quality of the journals and thus of the scholarship published in them to be of inferior quality to that published in traditional subscription-based journals. This was important because it meant that the work a scholar published in an open-access journal did not carry as much weight in promotion and tenure decisions as did work published in traditional journals. This perception has since become substantially less prevalent, although it still exists, partly because the actual quality of these journals improved through the use of peer review but partly because of the efforts of open-access advocates to educate scholars and administrators about it. Many open-access journals are now as prestigious as traditional journals, and most scholars now recognize that the quality of a scholarly journal cannot be determined simply by the format in which it is published or the price paid for a subscription but rather must be measured by the quality of the articles it publishes.

Tenure and Promotion

Tenure and promotion are the means by which scholars in institutions of higher education, that is, most scholars, advance in their careers. Untenured faculty members are on probation in their jobs until they achieve tenure, usually about seven years into their careers at an institution. Tenure means that scholars are granted a permanent position at the institution from which they cannot be removed except in extenuating circumstances. It originally developed as a means of providing scholars security in their jobs even if they disagreed publicly with or espoused ideas that were not held by the administrators of the institution; it guaranteed scholars freedom of speech without repercussion.

Tenure and promotion in institutions of higher education are granted on the basis of the quality and quantity of the scholar's work in some combination of research, teaching, and voluntary service to the institution, the community, and the scholar's discipline. The quality of the scholars' research is very often judged by the venues in which they communicate research results; hence, the phrase "publish or perish" is often applied to scholars on the tenure track. The scholarly journal is a prime venue for publishing research results. It is highly regarded because most work that is published in scholarly journals is peer-reviewed, as described earlier as reviewed or vetted by the researchers' peers as well as the editors of the journals. The more prestigious the scholarly journal in which it is published, the more weight a scholar's research is given in promotion and tenure decisions.

So it is clear that there is great incentive for scholars to publish the results of their research in scholarly journals that are held in high regard by those in the position to make tenure decisions. If, for instance, the decision makers are of the opinion that open-access journals are substandard, then there is little incentive for scholars to publish in them. This was and is still the case and was one of the reasons that open access and electronic journals faced an uphill battle for acceptance. Since scholarly journals are at the heart of the process of scholarly communication, the influence of the system of promotion and tenure in institutions of higher education on the process of scholarly communication is clear.

Public Policy

Chapter 9 discussed the influence that public policy can have on issues related to preservation of electronic resources. Public policy also has influence on the process of scholarly communication. During the past two decades, the policies that describe how government funds may be used for financial support of research have had a strong influence on the process of scholarly communication and the continued existence of open access. In particular, the NIH now stipulates that all reports of research funded by NIH be made freely and openly available to the public within 12 months of their publication in a peer-reviewed journal. The forum for making articles open access is PubMed Central, "a free full-text archive of biomedical and life sciences journal literature at the U.S. National Institutes of Health's National Library of Medicine" containing 3.5 million articles (U.S. National Library of Medicine and National Institutes of Health 2015).

Another source of public policy influence on the process of scholarly communication is the actions taken by the faculties of public universities to support open access by requiring faculty members to deposit a copy of their published scholarship in the institution's repository or archive. Institutional repositories are open-access initiatives instituted for the public good. For example, in 2013, the University of California Academic Senate voted into existence a policy that ensures that "research articles authored by faculty at all 10 campuses of UC will be made available to the public at no charge" (University of California Office of Scholarly Communication 2015). The policy requires that authors reserve the right to deposit a copy of their scholarly works in the UC repository whether it was originally published in an open-access journal or a subscription journal article in the institutional repository. It contains a provision for implementing an embargo, a delay before a publication is made available to the public, but not for opting out of compliance with the policy. Many private universities have also implemented open-access policies; one of the first was Harvard University.

SCHOLARLY COMMUNICATION AND THE MANAGEMENT OF ELECTRONIC RESOURCES

The process of scholarly communication is clearly intertwined with the management of electronic resources. In addition to being a major player in the process of scholarly communication themselves, libraries have as their customers and stakeholders all of the other major players. Scholars not only create the content of the electronic resources to which libraries subscribe, they are also some of the heaviest users of them and thus drive library collection development decisions. Publishers are often also electronic resource vendors, and if they are not, they are at the very least the controllers of the content, for instance, in the form of collections of scholarly journals included in vendor resources. Of the three other major players, librarians may have the least firsthand contact with funders and funding agencies, but because of the growing influence of funders and funding agencies on open access, of which librarians are often the strongest supporters on campus, often being charged with the implementation, growth, and management of institutional repositories, they are still clearly and closely related. So it should come as no surprise that the *Core Competencies for Electronic Resources Librarians* makes clear that electronic resource librarians should be "Committed to maintaining knowledge of current issues and trends in scholarly communication" (NASIG Core Competencies Task Force 2013, 7).

Chapter 11 will explore some potential trends and, perhaps, changes in the role the electronic resource librarian will play in the future of the system of scholarly communication.

ACTIVITY

1. What other examples of specific public policies can you think of that influence the process of scholarly communication? Describe the influence you see and support your argument.

REFERENCES

"Budapest Open Access Initiative." 2002. Retrieved from http://www.budapestope naccessinitiative.org/read.

Morrison, Heather. 2009. *Scholarly Communication for Librarians*. Oxford: Chandos.

NASIG Core Competencies Task Force. 2013. Core Competencies for Electronic Resources Librarians. NASIG. Retrieved from http://www.nasig.org/uploaded_files/92/files/CoreComp/CompetenciesforERLibrarians_final_ver_2013-7-22.pdf.

Radom, Rachel, Melanie Feltner-Reichert, and Kynita Stringer-Stanback. 2012. *Organization of Scholarly Communication Services, SPEC Kit 332 (November 2012)*. SPEC Kit 332. Washington, DC: Association of Research Libraries. Retrieved from http://publications.arl.org/Organization-of-Scholarly-Communication-Services-SPEC-Kit-332/.

Reitz, Joan. 2015. *ODLIS: Online Dictionary of Library and Information Science*. Retrieved from http://lu.com/odlis/search.cfm.

Swan, Alma. 2006. "1—Overview of Scholarly Communication." In *Open Access*, edited by Neil Jacobs, 3–12. Chandos Information Professional Series. Chandos Publishing. Retrieved from http://www.sciencedirect.com/science/article/pii/B9781843342038500017.

University of California Office of Scholarly Communication. 2015. "UC Open Access Policy." Office of Scholarly Communication University of California. Accessed June 21. Retrieved from http://osc.universityofcalifornia.edu/open-access-policy/.

U.S. National Library of Medicine, and National Institutes of Health. 2015. "PMC: PubMed Central." *PMC*. Accessed June 21. Retrieved from http://www.ncbi.nlm.nih.gov/pmc/.

Chapter 11
Future Directions of Electronic Resource Management

CONTENT

One of the most interesting, although perhaps not unusual, things about the development and evolution of electronic resources over the past two or three decades is how much they resemble their print counterparts. For instance, eBook functionality is based on print book functionality, readers navigate through content by "turning pages," even though the idea of a page has become amorphous and does not remain the same when the same book (manifestation) is read on different eBook readers. E-journal articles are still organized into volumes and issues and published "at regular or irregular intervals with no predetermined conclusion" (AACR and American Library 2002, chap. 12) even though there is no functional need to do so. The content, publication, functionality, and even business models for acquisition for electronic resources have, up to this point, remained quite similar to those for print resources. Perhaps this may be accounted for not only by the paths taken to develop the technological infrastructure but also by the users' need for some familiarity in order to make the transition from one format to another.

Manifestation is the name of one of four types of entities in the *Functional Rules for Bibliographic Records*. It refers to the idea of a book at

> the level at which it can be identified by having a unique ISBN but without the necessity of differentiating between copies with the same ISBN (Tillett 2004, 2)

But just as Web 1.0 evolved into Web 2.0, from passive viewing of static web pages to the ability for users to create their own content via social media and other applications, it seems only a matter of time before electronic information resources will evolve into formats that take advantage of the possibilities that new technologies afford. For example, it has been suggested that, as a result of linked data, within the next five years, journal content will no longer be constrained by the volume and issues organizational scheme used for the past 350 years but rather will become a "web of objects" (Van de Sompel 2014). It has also been suggested that within a slightly longer time frame, most scholarly content will be open access and that publishers' roles as providers of services like peer review, indexing, and search or retrieval platform design will become predominant (Rhind-Tutt 2015). It is also likely that electronic content delivery and use, especially of eBooks, will retain fewer of the functions and features of printed books and take on more of the useful functionality afforded by electronic access. Further, eBook acquisition and access models for libraries should do the same, for example, negating current frustrations with the "one-book, one-user" model still required by publishers in use in many libraries.

> Web 1.0 refers to the initial status of web-based content; it was static. Users could consume web-based content but not customize it, have bidirectional interactions with it, or create it.

> Web 2.0 is "a range of techniques used by internet-based systems that enable individuals to work more effectively with others. They enable the value of the internet to be enhanced by providing new opportunities for collaboration. Web 2.0 enables users to contribute to the content instead of only being a consumer" ("Web 2.0" 2013).

Linked-data "is an extension of the Semantic Web idea to reframe the basic principles of the Web's architecture in more semantic terms" (Glushko 2014, 672), that is to structure the web in a way that allows computers (rather than humans) to recognize relationships between things, like bibliographic records in library catalogs.

PRESERVATION

Issues of preservation are directly tied to form and functionality of content and therefore, in the face of the occurrences described in the preceding section, are also likely to continue to challenge librarians, publishers, and scholars alike. It is possible that these challenges may become more complex as a result of the availability and rapid adoption of multiple, more advanced storage formats and their subsequent obsolescence. But it may also be that the challenges of preserving the scholarly record in electronic formats will become less complex as content becomes increasingly platform neutral.

SCHOLARLY COMMUNICATION

As has been demonstrated in all of the preceding chapters, all of the issues and challenges, roles and responsibilities, and formats and functions of electronic resources make up a complex system in which both external and internal fluctuations create ripples of change. Given the future directions already mentioned in this chapter, it is no surprise that the process of scholarly communication is also likely to continue in flux, to be complex, and to change at a pace with changes in communication technology but to outpace changes in the rewards system.

TECHNOLOGY

It almost goes without saying that technology and the infrastructure surrounding the creation, acquisition, organization, delivery, and preservation of electronic resources will continue to surprise and amaze and, more importantly, to help libraries deliver more and better services to their customers. Single-sign on (SSO) technologies are likely to quickly become ubiquitous unless a simpler, better means of authentication is developed. Already institutions of higher education are using SSO to customize the institutional content that is delivered to visitors to their web pages. For instance, when faculty members use SSO to log in to the institutional site, they would be presented with information about faculty activities, advising and teaching related information, links to the human resources department, and, of course, library information and resource content related to their teaching and research interests. At the same time, students majoring in a subject such as business, upon using SSO to sign in to the institutional web page, might be presented with a schedule of business-related courses for the upcoming semester, the activities of business-related student organizations and clubs, financial aid information, and business-related library resources to which they would have access without the need to re-authenticate no matter where in the world they logged on from.

The results of technology advances on library electronic resource discovery, while there is no doubt of their existence, are slightly more difficult to predict. Discovery services already mimic web-based discovery, which many library customers find comforting and helpful but which some librarians believe minimizes the differences between natural language searching and more sophisticated search querying. While the former adequately serves most library customers, the existence of the latter is of great importance to a small, but important group of library customers, scholars, and researchers. However, it may also be the case that advances in semantic technology, the Semantic Web, and linked data may render this issue moot.

ELECTRONIC RESOURCE LIBRARIAN COMPETENCIES

It is not likely that the era of flush library budgets of the 1980s will ever again exist. Librarians are much more likely to continue to be faced with difficult decisions about which electronic resources to acquire. Further, the pressure to justify not only funds spent on resource acquisition but also their continued existence is only likely to increase as demands on institutional and governmental budgets increase.

Traditionally, electronic resource management has been the purview mainly of academic libraries by virtue of their relatively large collections of electronic resources compared with other types of libraries. This is slowly changing and is likely to continue to do so. Public and school libraries in particular are acceding to customer demands for more electronic content from eBooks and audiobooks to streaming video and gaming. Thus it is likely that the influence of public and other types of libraries on the life cycle of electronic resources and on many of the issues and challenges mentioned in this book will increase. As this occurs, the competencies required of electronic resource librarians as well as of those whose titles do not reflect their responsibilities for electronic resources management are likely to evolve as well.

Although the need for electronic resource librarians to be able to thrive in an environment of ambiguity and constant change is not likely to lessen, their responsibilities may evolve. One possible scenario is that a new intermediary position in libraries devoted to license and contract negotiation will begin to appear. The current situation, that is, the need for librarians to have substantial responsibilities in an area in which they are not professionally trained, for instance, contract law, is not sustainable. An alternative to a new position, one that is already occurring in some academic libraries, would be that such responsibility is farmed out to institutional legal counsel or purchasing specialists.

Indeed, the responsibilities and concurrent competencies related to work with electronic resources are so many and varied that in many libraries they are shared among multiple library staff. This makes it easy to imagine that the job of electronic resource librarian could become less ad hoc in the near future. In all types of libraries, electronic resource librarians have traditionally worn many hats. In academic libraries, for instance, they have had responsibilities for cataloging, reference work, bibliographic instruction, and liaising with academic disciplines within the institution in addition to their responsibilities for managing electronic resources. It is easy to imagine that, as electronic resources management begins to take more of their time, these librarians will be assigned fewer adjacent responsibilities. Some larger libraries have already taken an alternative route to distributing responsibility for electronic resources management by distributing them in a way that mirrors traditional library organization, for example, separating acquisitions from cataloging, troubleshooting from conducting trials, and license negotiation from evaluation and assessment. Another alternative is to separate responsibilities based on content and to then separate content management from delivery management. As electronic resources continue to make up more and more of the content libraries provide to their customers, it will be interesting to see whether at some point the specialized electronic resource librarian position becomes more popular than that of the electronic resource librarian generalist.

REFERENCES

AACR, Joint Steering Committee for Revision of, and Association American Library. 2002. *Anglo-American Cataloguing Rules*. Ottawa; Chicago: Canadian Library Association; American Library Association.

Glushko, R. J. 2014. *The Discipline of Organizing: Professional Edition*. O'Reilly Media.

Herbert Van de Sompel—From a System of Journals to a Web of Objects. 2014. Retrieved from http://www.youtube.com/watch?v=YG184V4gCRs&feature=youtube_gdata_player.

Rhind-Tutt, Stephen. 2015. "Somewhere to Run to, Nowhere to Hide." Presented at the NASIG Annual Conference, Washington, DC, May 29.

Tillett, B. 2004. "What Is FRBR? A Conceptual Model for the Bibliographic Universe." Library of Congress. Retrieved from http://www.loc.gov/cds/downloads/FRBR.PDF.

"Web 2.0." 2013. *BCS Glossary of Computing and ICT*. Swindon, United Kingdom: BCS, The Chartered Institute for IT.

Index